Transformed:
Intimacy With God

Dear Lesa,
God bless you in
your intimate
walk with Him.
Ps. 46:10

Anthony J. Guadalatto
5/22/04

Transformed: Intimacy With God

Learn How to Be Still and Know
God Personally, Passionately, and
Powerfully

Dr. Anthony J. Fischetto

Alpha Omega Counseling Center, Inc.
Reading, Pennsylvania

TRANSFORMED: INTIMACY WITH GOD
Learn How to Be Still and Know God Personally, Passionately, and Powerfully

2004 Second Printing Revised and Expanded with Discussion Questions

Copyright © 2000 by Anthony J. Fischetto

Published by:

Alpha Omega Counseling Center, Inc.
Post Office Box 66
Reading, PA 19607 U.S.A.
Telephone: 610-777-3306, E-mail: afische101@aol.com

Front cover is a picture of God's radiance 30,000 feet above sea level taken by the author.
Front and back cover design by Patrick D. Stiles.
Back cover also designed by Christopher Coleman.

Publisher's Cataloging in Publication
Fischetto, Anthony
Transformed: Intimacy With God—Learn How to Be Still and Know God Personally, Passionately, and Powerfully/ Anthony Fischetto
    p. cm.
    1. Spiritual renewal. 2. Meditation. 3. Transformation. 4. Intimacy with God. I. Title.

Library of Congress Control Number: 00-091011

ISBN 0-9678697-0-6 (softcover)

Printed in the United States of America

To my parents,
Anthony and Connie,
and my four sisters
Millie, Jeanette,
Connie, and Julie,
who have shown me
consistency in their
love for me
throughout my life.

CONTENTS

Acknowledgments

My deep appreciation to all the people for their contribution in completing this book.

My thanks and gratitude to the following people for their many devoted hours and weeks of laborious work in typing, making suggestions, editing, proofreading, and continual encouragement: Chris Ann Ceraso, JoAnne Earnest, Sue Pernice, Heidi Zengel, and Denise Techmeier.

Many others have helped me in the writing process of this book in various ways and have given support for which I am very grateful: Jeff Custer (evangelist at the Shillington Church of Christ), Scott Russell, Rick Ryan, Avery D. Miller, Elaine Allen, Laurie Shircy, Becky Lee, Becky Daniels, Irene Powers, Kathy Politzer, Patrick D. Stiles (front and back cover designer), Terri Clemen, Billy Knigge (my nephew), John W. Smith (an editor of the *Reading Eagle* newspaper), Gordon Burgett (a book editor), Dr. Earnest Rossi (for his ultradian research), Tom Pernice, Georgia Buchert (the church secretary), Kaye Nicol, Sue Myers and Deidra Schaefer (from BookMasters, Inc.), Sue Easter, James D. McKinney, the Shillington Church of Christ, and many others.

Most of all, I thank God who allows me to be in his almighty, loving presence through Jesus Christ my Lord and who fills me with his Holy Spirit.

Introduction

Do you feel worn out and fatigued? Do you feel empty and dry? Do you feel like you are just spinning your wheels without advancing? Do you feel rushed and hurried much of your time, with little rest? Do you feel weak physically, emotionally, or mentally? The problem may be that you are no longer growing spiritually and that your personal relationship with God no longer seems real.

You're searching for more in life, while at the same time you have to force yourself to read the Bible or pray. However, reading the Bible is like reading the telephone book, and spiritual exercises have become boring. "Well," you might say, "I do go to church. I read my Bible. I pray. My church is a loving, praising church. I'm involved in ministries, but I'm still feeling 'blah' spiritually. I just don't have the passion. I just don't feel really connected." What's wrong? You actually are longing for spiritual joy but can't seem to find it. You may realize that this is the problem because you feel envious of someone else's faith and joy in Christ, or you may not realize this and just view your spiritual weariness as a symptom of a greater problem.

There is no greater problem than spiritual weariness. When we are spiritually weary, we are bound to experience these physical and emotional symptoms of a spiritual dysfunction. We all experience some of these symptoms at times. This is a great danger because you are more prone to be ineffective and unproductive in your faith and life (2 Peter 1:5-11) and at a greater risk of falling from your faith (2 Peter 1:10). Being spiritually weak can lead to physical, emotional, mental, or spiritual problems and an actual tendency to supplement your faith with destructive things of the world. You may look for love in all the wrong places and become sexually impure in your thoughts and actions. You may become depressed from loneliness and despair and have feelings of helplessness and hopelessness.

Instead of giving our problems to God and trusting in him, we try to escape them in many ways. We escape through such things as alcohol, drugs, sex, food, television, and work. We may even try to escape through positive activities such as church activities and ministry work. However, if we are not depending on God's guidance and strength, we will grow weak. If we do not seek God's agenda but only do our own agenda, we will burnout. In our society, we tend to be too self-centered, self-absorbed, and self-indulgent. We have been greatly influenced by secular humanism where humankind is the center of all strength and hope instead of God. Many people are flocking to New Age methods, which make them their own god. However, God is still our creator and maker, and so he knows best how to make us joyful. God is active and alive!

God wants to help us. Jesus says to us now, "Here I am! I stand at the door and knock. If anyone hears my voice and opens the door, I will come in and eat with him and he with me" (Rev. 3:20). We must remember that true transformation into a life of peace is not by our might or power, but by God's power, which comes from his Spirit (Zech. 4:6).

Are you ready to be renewed, revived, refreshed, rejuvenated, revitalized, relaxed, and re-awakened to the beauty, power, and majesty of God our creator?

Our true transformation does not come by our own attempts at self-actualization. It doesn't come by spicing up the church services or by trying to perk up our lives with things or activities. The problem in our lives is noise, distractions, and too much busyness. More and more people say they are too busy to spend time with God. Remember what Jesus says, "Come with me by yourselves to a quiet place and get some rest" (Mark 6:31). You must come to Jesus and spend quality, quiet time with him to find rest and to be restored and revived physically, emotionally, and spiritually. Jesus says:

> Come to me, all you who are weary and burdened, and I will give you rest. Take my yoke upon you and learn from me, for I am gentle and humble in heart, and you will find rest for your souls. For my yoke is easy and my burden is light. (Matt. 11:28-29)

Paul wrote, "And we, who with unveiled faces all reflect the Lord's glory, are being transformed into His likeness with ever increasing glory, which comes from the Lord, who is in the Spirit" (2 Cor. 3:18). We are being transformed with God's *glory*! This means that we will have direct benefits in every part of our lives, including spiritual, physical, and emotional transformations into joy and peace with God.

Spiritual Benefits

Spiritually, you will develop a deeper, personal, and intimate relationship with God based on his unconditional love. Your fears and worries will be dissolved. Perfect love casts out all fears (I John 4:18). Your confidence and trust in God will strengthen. You will be more effective and productive in your Christian walk. You will live a more victorious Christian life with a greater peace. You will be a more loving, caring, accepting, and forgiving Christian. You will want to share Christ's love with others and lead them to Christ for full salvation.

Physical Benefits

Physically, you will be more relaxed and less stressed. Stress is a major problem in our world today and contributes to numerous health problems. The risk of stress-related illnesses such as heart disease, high blood pressure, a weakened immune system, injuries, colds, chronic fatigue syndrome, fibromyalgia, obesity, ulcers, and countless other ailments can be reduced as a result of your journey with Christ.

Emotional Benefits

Emotionally, you can feel more confident, secure, and balanced. As you develop a deeper, more personal, trusting, and intimate relationship with God, you will feel more accepted for who you are as a unique individual created by God who loves you unconditionally. Moreover, as the best-selling author Max Lucado says, "We must understand that there is nothing we can do to increase or diminish God's love!" [1] However, we must find a way to really accept and experience God's unconditional love that is waiting for us. Experiencing God and his love can help us overcome our feelings of loneliness, depression, anxiety, desperation, addictions, confusion, doubt, sadness, worries, and selfishness.

The key is learning how to be still in order to experience God's mighty presence and to trust him: Psalm 37:7 and Psalm 46:10.

Practical and Unique

This is a practical book to help aid your transformation into the likeness of God. This book differs from most of the teachings in our society that tell you to do more to achieve success. Even in the church, when you want greater transformation and to improve your relationship with God, they tell you to do more—more praying, more Bible reading, go to church more, believe more, get more involved, go to some spiritual training programs, and other means to be reconnected with God. All these things are good and are essential—and most of us need to do these things more.

However, I believe the key to transformation is to set aside time to be intimate with God in quietness. Keep in mind; the transformation does not come from us. Therefore, we need to learn how to set aside everything at times and just sit still with God. This is very difficult for most people. We are conditioned to go, work, and push ourselves in order to be successful. We need to learn to let go, slow down, take a break from our own efforts and be still before the Great Almighty God and Creator of the Universe. It is only then that we can enter into the deep spiritual intimacy with God. It is in this special holy, personal time that we can be recharged and renewed for his glory. Then we are more able to go back to our lives and apply God's power to our difficult situations and to be more activated to do his will. This book not only describes the importance of being still, but also shows you how to be still before God—allowing God to do the transforming.

An Inside Glimpse of the Book

May your whole spirit, soul and body be kept blameless at the coming of our Lord Jesus Christ.
(1 Thess. 5:23)

The principles I've written in this book deal with the whole person—body (physical), soul (emotional), and spirit (spiritual). It is designed to help you explore practical ways to achieve a greater stillness with God, teaching you how to experience the presence of God, so he can transform your whole self. These principles and approaches in being still before God and knowing him intimately and more personally have transformed my life and continue to do so daily as I depend on him. It is a lifelong process. I am in continual need for God's transforming power.

Together we will:

1. Study the Scriptures' teachings on biblical meditation in both the Old and New Testament.

2. Study the lives of biblical people who had intimate relationships with God and learn from them.

3. Examine the physical and biological aspects of biblical meditation, understand how God designed us to be intimate with him, and apply the newly discovered science of ultradian rhythms.

4. Employ self-examination tools to help us focus on God more.

5. Explore the emotional and spiritual dimensions of Christian meditation.

6. Look at the fourfold human response of *awareness*, *conviction (trembling)*, *healing (transformation)*, and *calling to personal mission*.

7. Study the spiritual disciplines that are interconnected with Christian meditation, such as prayer, fasting, and Bible reading.

8. Apply these spiritual disciplines to prepare us for an "out-of-this-world" encounter with the living God.

The presence of the almighty God can create a powerful impact on those who enter into a deeper relationship with him. Be prepared for the strong emotional and spiritual changes that often result from increased intimacy with God.

An audiocassette is also available. The tape is a 20-minute guided walk into the presence of Jesus while being still with him that will allow his spirit to transform you according to God's will. Always remember that you are the clay; he is the potter. The tape is a 20-minute relaxation tape with Jesus in following his command in Mark 6:31 to come away with him by yourself to a quiet place and get some rest.

My Prayer

My prayer is for you to enjoy greater intimacy and passion with our loving God, that your relationship with the Lord will grow by applying the principles in this book to your life.

I pray that you will allow him to continually transform you into his image. Join me now in our journey to greater intimacy and transformation with God.

Enjoy your quiet time with God.
Allow him to transform you.

I

The Key
to
Transformation

1

God Transformed My Switchblade Into a Sword

If I could have but one of my heart's desires granted in my lifetime, it would be for everyone in God's world to be transformed, made new in his image—to convince the human race that dramatic personal transformation is possible for all! Even if you feel as if you are a lost cause, I believe that if God could transform me, he can do the same for you!

What I'm about to share with you is the part of my past of which I am the least proud. I regret that my actions and lifestyle dishonored God. However, I write this in the hope that you, too, will come to place greater faith in God and let his power change your life.

Growing up, for me on Long Island, New York, in the mid 1970s was a wild time. I was involved with the "wrong" teen crowd—drinking, doing drugs, and joining fraternities, some of which were more like gangs. Running from the police was a common occurrence.

I remember one instance when I was frantically fleeing on my illegal motorcycle. Wearing no helmet and having no license with which to drive, with nothing but the immaturity of youth to guide me, I led police on a chase, which took me through most of my neighborhood. When I finally beat a path across the narrow strip of property between two houses, I knew I was safe. The strip of ground was too narrow for a police cruiser to follow me. This was a very stressful and fearful experience.

Another dark moment in my life was on one late Saturday night when I was sixteen. The police surprised my gang of friends, scattering us in different directions. As I ran, searching for a good place to hide, I remember ditching my switchblade, nunchaks, and other miscellaneous items that the police would not appreciate.

Ironically, I ended up outside of a Catholic church—but not just any Catholic church. This was the same one that I had attended as a child. This was where I had learned my catechism on Wednesday afternoons after school, where I had made my first communion, and where I had taken my confirmation. Yep, the very same church I had visited on special occasions like Christmas and Easter. Now I was back!

I was frightened and needed a place to hide, so I slipped into the building with two of my partners in crime close behind me. (Today I joke that even then I was leading people into church!) We crept into the candlelit sanctuary, and my two friends immediately hid under the pews, but not me. I wanted a safer place. I ducked behind the curtain of one of the confessionals and squatted down in the darkened corner of the booth still breathing heavy from the chase, my heart still racing. I felt irreverent, using this place of worship for a hideout.

All of a sudden I heard the dreaded sound of someone coming down the aisle! My heart began to beat faster as the echoing steps got closer. I had been convinced that no one would know where I was hiding, or would they?

I peered out from under the curtain of the confessional booth and watched in horror as two shiny black shoes stopped in front of my hiding place.

In one swift motion, a hand threw back the curtain and reached into the darkness, grabbing me by the arm! It was the resident parish priest! He had also rounded up my two friends, and within seconds, he threw all of us out of the building and back onto the street! But by that time, the police had stopped searching for us. We did escape the authorities that night, but we continued living on the edge.

I soon became increasingly dissatisfied with the wild life. It was in reality dreary, destructive, hurtful, miserable, and empty. I began longing for something better. Those two years were the darkest period of my life. I felt hopeless and helpless, and I was losing the will to live.

Even though I was involved in many destructive activities, there was always a deep spiritual element inside of me crying out for a new life. Gradually this spiritual concern began to grow within me as I realized how my wild teen life was empty and meaningless. Therefore, my wild escapades soon began to diminish. If I were to stay my final year in high school, it would be wasted on continuous partying. Desiring to move ahead with my life, I decided to graduate early by doubling up on my classes in the eleventh grade. After the eleventh grade, I started college. More importantly, I began my search for a greater meaning to my life.

Now that I look back, I regret having put my parents through those tumultuous years of my life. I have a newfound respect for what they dealt with. Although they had raised me to believe in God and had taught me to pray, I still disobeyed not only them, but God as well. I had to hit rock bottom to be motivated to seek a new life.

The Turning Point

On the campus of the State University of New York where I attended, there was a yoga-meditation class. The description of the class made it sound inviting. Therefore, I decided to try it as a non-Christian at this time. Although I enjoyed the classes, an essential element of life seemed to be missing from the yoga meditations. I soon left the yoga-meditation practice, and instead learned to meditate on God in the biblical way. At the same time, I was experiencing a growing faith in God and coming to know Jesus Christ more personally. I decided to modify the meditation practice every day at home by meditating on Jesus. I would sit in silence and meditate on God with a booklet of scriptures that I had found. As my passion for God began to grow, I realized that it was exactly what I had been searching for all along.

Rays of sunlight began to break through the darkness in my soul. I prayed for God to show me his way, and I began searching for people who followed the teachings of the Bible as God had intended.

In 1978, during a campus Bible study, I was thrilled to receive a Bible of my own. I remember the joy and excitement I felt as I read God's Word. I could hardly put it down. I remember making time to have intense, focused, personal time with God every day in these early days of my spiritual enlightenment.

As I read how the Word of God is the sword of the Holy Spirit (Eph. 6:17), it finally dawned on me that God had transformed my switchblade into a sword. Now I had a new weapon to use for a new battle. God had a plan for my life.

It has been over twenty years since I was baptized into Christ as an adult believer and follower of him. Yet throughout those twenty years, I have found that my relationship with God and the strength of my spiritual life still depend on how much intimate, quiet, and meditative time I spend with God. When I neglected my quiet times, it was usually because I was pulled away by the influences and cares of the world.

This book grows out of my passion to share this vitally important topic with you. Let me emphasize that these quiet times are *essential* for everyone who wants to know God personally, passionately, and powerfully. We see this discipline throughout the life of Jesus, as well as the great leaders who preceded him.

II

Do You Hear the Bridegroom Calling?

2

What Is God's Passion?

I know a man who strives to become a better husband. He reads books like *What Wives Wish Their Husbands Knew About Women* by Dr. James Dobson. He meets with other men to discuss ways of putting these theories into practice and to get pointers from their collective experiences. He goes to weekly lectures to learn even more. He helps around the house at times. He always gives his wife at least a quick kiss on the cheek before leaving for work in the morning, and gives her several brief phone calls sporadically throughout the day. He runs home from work for a quick bite to eat, only to rush back out to another meeting to learn how to be a better husband. He comes home late from his meeting, only to read another book on being a better husband. After reading, he gives his wife a kiss goodnight.

Is there anything wrong with this picture? Can you see what's missing? The one thing his wife wants most from her spouse is his time.

He is actually so busy learning how to be a better husband that he's missing the point. She wants to spend intimate time together, giving full attention to each other—no phones, no kids, no interruptions. They don't even have to talk with each other continually during this quiet time together. She just wants him to show his appreciation of her by holding her close. Basically, she wants him to know her deepest thoughts and desires. No matter how *much* the husband tries to improve himself, unless he gives his wife personal love and affection, he will not know his wife intimately. She may even question his motive for doing these things. Is he doing it for himself or for her?

Are not most Christians, including you and me, like this husband in regards to our daily Christian walk? Do we spend more time seeking godliness, rather than seeking God?

What is our motive for doing the right things? Do we study the Bible to gain greater knowledge or to hear what God has to say? Do we go to church more out of a sense of duty and peer pressure than for renewing our faith in Jesus? Why do we get involved with various church activities and ministries? Do we try to better ourselves as Christians, but lack a personal intimate love relationship with God?

Society teaches us to be more self-absorbed than God-absorbed, more self-centered than God-centered. The whole New Age movement teaches us how to become self-sufficient and to be our own gods. It promotes self-actualization and the saving of ourselves by our own abilities. Are we guilty of some sort of idolatry—worshipping the created rather than the Creator?

If you're like me, sometimes we need a wake-up call! Even though I was caught up in many exciting "religious" things, there have been times when I would drift from personal intimate time with God. Whatever my excuse, feeling too busy or too tired to sit still with God and to listen to him, conversing and praying to him, I found myself drifting ever so slowly away from what is vital and important. Does God give us wake-up calls? Yes! And we can hear them if we are in tune with him. Look at the specific wake-up call God gives through his prophet Isaiah:

Hear, O heavens! Listen, O earth! For the Lord has spoken. [Sounds like a wake-up call to me.] I have regarded my children and brought them up, but they have rebelled against me. The ox knows his master, the donkey knows his owner's manger, but Israel does not know, my people do not understand. (Isa. 1:2-3)

"The multitude of your sacrifices—what are they to me?" says the Lord. "I have more than enough of burnt offerings, I have no pleasure in the blood of bulls and lambs and goats." (Isa. 1:11)

"Stop bringing meaningless offerings!"(Isa. 1:13)

God is describing a vain form of worship here in which his people have drifted away from what God really wants from them.

To Know God Intimately

What does God want the most from his people Israel and still want from us? What is more important than our money, possessions, works, time, and man-made traditions? Answer: to know God intimately with our total being, like a husband knows his wife. Scripture refers to us as God's bride, his wife. (Read Hosea, Isa. 54:5-6; Jer. 2:2; Eph. 5; Rev. 19:7; 21:2, 9; 22:17) God's children are referred to as "the bride, the wife of the Lamb [Jesus Christ]" (Rev. 21:9). God knows if he has our heart, we will honor him with our lives. If God has our heart, all the rest will follow—we will trust and obey.

To Hear God and Listen

"Teacher, which is the greatest commandment in the Law?" Jesus replied, "Love the Lord your God with all your heart and with all your soul and with all your mind. And the second is like it: Love your neighbor as yourself. All the Law and the prophets hang on these two commandments." (Matt. 22:37-40)

In the above scripture, Jesus was quoting from Deuteronomy 6:4, which is referred to as the *Shema*, which is Hebrew for "Hear." God wants us to *hear* the important message he has for us.

Special News Report

Imagine yourself sitting in front of the TV watching your favorite show when the broadcast is interrupted for a special news report. The newsperson warns you to watch your children carefully because someone in the neighborhood has been kidnapping children by luring them away with exciting toys and games. The children become so stimulated by these toys and games that they forget all about what their parents have taught them about strangers. Their focus changes completely, and it's very difficult to get the children to remember their parents once this happens.

How would you, as a parent, react to such a report? I believe that you would respond with great concern, warning your children again of "stranger-danger" and keeping a closer eye on them as they play outside.

Well, God is sending a special news report that demands our full attention. He's saying:

SPECIAL NEWS BULLETIN!
My children have been lured away from their true parent by the "exciting" things of this world. I will be searching for them until the last one is found!

God wants us to know him intimately so that nothing will entice us away from him or lead us into destructive ways. He tells us to *"Hear,"*and to *"Listen"* to him, for he has spoken (Isa. 1:2).

Over the last several years, I have asked hundreds of people to share the one key way to become more intimate with another person. Almost everyone I asked gave me the same answer. The key is "to spend time with that person."

God designed us to crave this intimate relationship with him since the beginning of time. In the beginning, God had this type of relationship with Adam and Eve before they sinned when he walked with them in the Garden of Eden (Gen. 2 and 3).

After this close relationship with individuals failed, God chose the community of Israel to be his own and to have an intimate relationship with him. God calls the Israelites his children—and he chose them to be the vehicle for sending the Savior, his own Son, into the world.

However, the Jewish nation rebelled against their Father and began to worship their own abilities, intellect, strength, and position. Their religious worship became an empty, mechanical, ritualistic formula. The Israelites thought that by doing all the "right" things in formal worship that they would automatically be blessed.

But God himself said through the prophet Isaiah, "These people come near to me with their mouth and honor me with their lips, but their hearts are far from me. Their worship of me is made up only of rules taught by men" (Isa. 29:13). These people drifted far from the one who can and wants to give them everything.

Even Jesus pointed out to the same Jewish nation 700 years later that although they "diligently study the Scriptures...think[ing] that by them [they] possess eternal life...yet [they] refuse to come to me to have life" (John 5:39-40). They continued to miss the point.

Two thousand years later, human nature still has not changed. We miss the point if we miss knowing God on a personal level through Jesus. As John confronted the Ephesians some 60 years after Jesus' life on earth, have we also *drifted away from our first love*? (Rev. 2:4-5).

God says, "The ox knows his master, and the donkey knows his owner's manger" (Isa.1: 3). Isn't it interesting that God compares his wayward children to two of the least intelligent animals in his creation? Certain commentaries call the ox and the donkey "brute beasts" and the most stupid of all animals. Yet these beasts acknowledge their master; they know who feeds them and takes care of them, unlike God's own children.

Jesus asked of the apostle Peter, "Do you love me?" (John 21:17). We need to ask ourselves, "Do we love Jesus?" And our answer will really be found in how much intimate, personal time we spend with him. Do we have an ongoing love affair with God?

Nothing else will suffice. Nothing else will give us eternal life, meaning, purpose, satisfaction, or true joy. Only Jesus! Nothing else! Does that mean we should live in a cave and meditate on Jesus without doing anything else? Certainly not! Being intimate with God through Jesus Christ means that we will be transformed into the likeness of God—full of compassion, humility, obedience, and service to God and to others. This active transformation gives us a confidence inside us, knowing we are fully loved, peaceful from having spent time with his spirit, and capable of meeting the world with his strengths of compassion, humility, and service to God. Just as a husband's support enables a wife to feel that she can tackle anything, God's love and guidance enables his bride to carry his joy to others. Times of loving intimacy are such an important blessing in either relationship.

Jesus plainly stated in the great commandment, "Love the Lord your God with all your heart and with all your soul and with all your mind." We must achieve head knowledge, heart knowledge, and soul knowledge of God through Jesus Christ his Son and from his Holy Spirit. Then we can more readily love our neighbor as ourselves (Matt. 22:37-40).

Is God calling you by name to come to him just as you are, to be restored, renewed and transformed?

This is his passion!

3

Biblical Meditation

It has been said, "A way to a man's heart is through his stomach." Men tend to be satisfied by physical things—food, sex, gadgets, and cars. Women tend to be satisfied by relational things—love, affection, and attention. God is satisfied when we surrender our entire selves—physically, relationally, and spiritually.

We have seen in Chapter two how God longs for our total love and devotion to him. Now we want to learn more of God's way to our heart. How does God connect with our heart and fulfill his desire? How can we connect with God?

God's Way to Our Heart

God desires our full and undivided attention continually. This may sound a little extreme, but we see in Scripture how God is a jealous God. We are not to divide our attention with other gods. This is the second commandment.

> You shall not bow down to them or worship them; for I, the LORD your God, am a jealous God. (Exod. 20:5)

Do not worship any other god, for the LORD, whose name is Jealous, is a jealous God. (Exod. 34:14)

For the LORD your God is a consuming fire, a jealous God. (Deut. 4:24)

You shall not bow down to them or worship them; for I, the LORD your God, am a jealous God. (Deut. 5:8-9)

Joshua said to the people, "You are not able to serve the LORD. He is a holy God; he is a jealous God." (Josh. 24:19)

God wants our full heart. Jesus says that we cannot serve two masters or we will love one and hate the other (Matt. 6:24). James says we cannot be a friend of the world and a friend of God. We must choose whom we will serve (James 4:4).

But what does it mean to give God our full attention? It means to have times of concentrated focus on God where we filter out all distractions. This includes Bible study, going to church, and all the other typical thought of things. It also includes meditation through contemplating, reflecting, remembering, and absorbing who God is, what he says to us, and how we reply back to him.

Now, before you reject this concept either by thinking negatively about the concept of meditation, by thinking this is too "New Age," too mystical, is for monks only, or is only for people who have time for this type of thing—let's look at what God says about meditation.

Definition:
Meditation means to deliberately reflect, concentrate, or focus on some subject.

God is the subject of our affections in biblical meditation. The word meditation comes from two different Hebrew words (haghuth and sichah). [1] These two words are used fifty-eight times in the Bible. [2] These words are defined by meditating on God's word, works, or wonders. The author Richard Foster describes the various meanings as "listening to God's word, reflecting on God's works, rehearsing God's deeds, ruminating on God's law, and more." [3] It is closely connected with solitude and prayer.

Why Does God Want Us to Meditate?

God wants us to meditate on him because it is his key to our heart. King David was a man after God's own heart, and David meditated on God day and night:

> But his delight is in the law of the LORD, and on his law he meditates day and night. (Ps. 1:2)

As a young shepherd boy in the fields, David must have spent a lot of time gazing at the stars in the sky, praising God. He had much time to be still and quiet to realize the glory of God.

David could have been closer to God than all the other religious leaders. Maybe that's why he appeared to have a greater faith when he volunteered to go up against Goliath. David knew his God personally, and God knew David. Don't you want that kind of relationship with God? I do!

We show our love to God by recognizing his majesty and power all around us and giving him the glory (Ps. 19). However, the noise and distractions in our busy world dim our view and muffle our hearing from the presence of God. Meditation helps us focus on God with greater attention and affection. We become more conscious of his presence to the point that even the mundane things in our life become meaningful because God is there with us. This pleases God and touches his heart.

A child sits in front of her father, and listens intently to his story. When her father finishes the story, she says, "Daddy, tell me more, tell me more!" This child is meditating on her father and is excited to hear him talking to her. She feels love and acceptance. The other kids are running around outside playing and making a lot of noise. They can't hear their daddy and seldom take the time to do so. They don't know what they are missing.

According to author Elmer L. Towns, "Learning the discipline of meditation is your key element to building a better life for his glory."[4] How does God want us to meditate? The Bible mentions meditating on God's word, works and wonders.

Meditate on His Word

Do not let this *Book of the Law* depart from your mouth; *meditate* on it day and night, so that you may be careful to do everything written in it. Then you will be prosperous and successful. (Josh. 1:8, emphasis mine)

I *meditate* on your *precepts* and consider your ways. (Ps. 119:15, emphasis mine)

Though rulers sit together and slander me, your servant will *meditate* on your *decrees*. (Ps. 119:23, emphasis mine)

I lift up my hands to your commands, which I love, and I *meditate* on your *decrees*. (Ps. 119:48, emphasis mine)

May the arrogant be put to shame for wrongdoing me without cause; but I will *meditate* on your *precepts*. (Ps. 119:78, emphasis mine)

Oh, how I love your *law*! I *meditate* on it all day long. (Ps. 119:97, emphasis mine)

I have more insights than all your teachers, for I *meditate* on your *statutes*. (Ps. 119:99, emphasis mine)

My eyes stay open through the watches of the night, that I may *meditate* on your *promises*. (Ps. 119:148, emphasis mine)

We are required to do more than just read God's Word superficially. We are to *let the Word of Christ dwell in us richly* (Col. 3:15, emphasis mine), and as Joshua wrote in the first quotation, we will be successful if we obey God's Word.

Read a portion of the Bible, stop, reflect on what God is saying to you from his word, and let your mind and heart be renewed by the Word.

Meditate on His Works

I will *meditate* on all your *works* and consider all your mighty deeds. (Ps. 77:12, emphasis mine)

I remember the days of long ago; I *meditate* on all your *works* and consider what your hands have done. (Ps. 143:5, emphasis mine)

We are strengthened in our faith and renewed in our love for God as we remember and meditate on what he has done. He created the entire universe and everything in it. Spend time like David and stare into the starry sky. Consider how, "the heavens declare the glory of God; the skies proclaim the *work* of his hands" (Ps. 19:1, emphasis mine).

The following are some glorious works of God on which to meditate and give him the praise and honor:

Sunrises	The vast blue sky
Sunsets	The majestic mountains
Changing color of leaves	The mighty ocean
The gentle flying butterfly	The cool gentle breezes
The beautiful spring flowers	The white fluffy clouds

His greatest work is what he accomplished on the cross through his Son Jesus Christ. He sacrificed his only Son so that we could have eternal life. This is what we are to meditate upon each time we partake of the Lord's Supper (the Holy Communion).

Meditate on His Wonders

Let me understand the teaching of your precepts; then I will *meditate* on your *wonders*. (Ps. 119:27, emphasis mine)

Remember the *wonders* he has done, his miracles, and the judgments he pronounced. (1 Chron. 16:12; Ps. 105:5, emphasis mine)

Listen to this, Job; stop and *consider* God's *wonders*. (Job 37:14, emphasis mine)

I will remember the works of the LORD; Surely I will *remember* your *wonders* of old. (Ps. 77:11 NKJV, emphasis mine)

The words remembering, considering, and meditating can be used interchangeably. We give our focused attention through meditation on God's wonders he has done throughout all time. What wonders has God done in your life such as saving you through certain situations, giving you loving friends or family, answering your prayers in times of need, and providing for your needs. Meditate on the wonders God has done in your life and in the life of others, and be ready for God to give you peace and comfort. We serve an awesome God.

Jesus Tells Us to Meditate

Come with me by yourselves to a quiet place and get some rest. (Mark 6:31)

Come to me, all you who are weary and burdened, and I will give you rest. Take my yoke upon you and learn from me, for I am gentle and humble in heart, and you will find rest for your souls. For my yoke is easy and my burden is light. (Matt. 11:28-30)

Jesus himself knew the need for physical, emotional, and spiritual rest. Jesus often went away to a quiet place to rest and to pray. Naturally, he wanted to share this with us.

Very early in the morning, while it was still dark, Jesus got up, left the house and went off to a solitary place, where he prayed. (Mark 1:35)

But Jesus often withdrew to lonely places and prayed. (Luke 5:16)

One of those days Jesus went out to a mountainside to pray, and spent the night praying to God. When morning came, he called his disciples to him. (Luke 6:12-13)

Immediately Jesus made his disciples get into the boat and go on ahead of him to Bethsaida, while he dismissed the crowd. After leaving them, he went up on a mountainside to pray. (Mark 6:45-46)

After he had dismissed them, he went up on a mountainside by himself to pray. When evening came, he was there alone. (Matt 14:23-24)

Once when Jesus was praying in private and his disciples were with him, he asked them, "Who do the crowds say I am?" (Luke 9:18)

About eight days after Jesus said this, he took Peter, John and James with him and went up onto a mountain to pray. (Luke 9:28)

Then, because so many people were coming and going that they did not even have a chance to eat, he said to them, "Come with me by yourselves to a quiet place and get some rest." (Mark 6:31)

If Jesus needed to get away to spend quiet, meditative time with his Father in prayer and solitude, how much more do we need to?

Benefits of Meditation and Solitude

Supernatural Benefits

1. You become more intimate with God.
2. You improve your relationship with God.

3. You improve your relationship with others.
4. You are able to rise above your problems with greater hope and joy.
5. You are transformed into the image of God (2 Cor. 3:18).
6. You can deal better with life's problems.
7. You become more in tune with God.
8. You quiet the noise and distraction to hear and see God better.
9. You transform your will into his will.
10. You become one with God as Jesus prayed (John 17).
11. You rise above the superficialities in your spiritual walk.
12. You are empowered by God to walk more by faith and not by sight.

Natural Benefits

1. You reduce the negative effects of stress.
2. You can reduce your blood pressure.
3. You can improve your blood circulation.
4. You improve your sleep.
5. You increase your energy.
6. You can relieve headaches.
7. You can improve heart disease.
8. You can relax and calm yourself in anxious situations.
9. You can help your natural healing process.
10. You help your immune system.
11. You can develop more patience.

We do not practice Christian meditation for our physical or natural benefits, but rather for God's benefit. This is where he wants our hearts—one with his (John 17). But just as earthly human intimacy blesses us in so many ways, so does Godly intimacy.

A Moment with Him

We mutter and sputter,
We fume and we spurt:
We mumble and grumble,
Our feelings get hurt:
We can't understand things,
Our vision grows dim,
When all that is needed is
A moment with Him.

Author unknown

4

Are You a Martha or a Mary?

The Importance of Listening

A friend called the other day while I was working on my computer. She was sharing a story with me but I was only half listening, because I was still working on my computer. Throughout the conversation (if you could call it that), I would occasionally mumble a word of acknowledgement in response to something she said. "Yeah...mmh...oh really...that's nice." However, it was clear that I really was not listening, but was rather distracted. Eventually, she asked me what I was doing. She could tell that she did not have my full attention. Obviously, she felt hurt.

When will I learn? I know how I feel when I want to talk to someone, and they are distracted by things they are doing and do not give me their full attention. We find it so difficult to just sit and listen without distractions.

We tend to get so overwhelmed with our daily activities, we might say, "When *do* we have the time to just sit and listen?" We are consumed with work, raising a family, washing clothes, cooking, doing yardwork, taking care of the kids' needs, going shopping, doing housework, and just being involved in so many other things. The list is endless. We tend to fantasize that someday things will slow down, but they seldom do. Often our lives get busier and even more rushed. We must ask ourselves what is so important about the "things" we have to do to the point of neglecting what really matters—relationships.

Many couples who come to me for marital counseling are on the verge of a divorce and have a few common regrets. They wished they spent more intimate time with each other, listened to each other more often, turned off the television, put down the newspaper, stayed awake, and paid more attention to each other. The familiar quote, "I have never heard anyone say on their deathbed, 'I wished I had spent more time at the office,'" aptly shows the regret many people feel when looking at how they chose to prioritize their life. The importance of giving our undivided attention is vital and essential if we want to develop a good relationship with someone.

Listening!

Listening is a lost art in our modern technical society. Although technology was supposed to make our life easier and give us more time, we have less time for the one thing needed in our lives—to sit at the feet of Jesus and listen. Listening is not an easy task. We tend to retain 40% or less of what we hear. For people to grasp your message, they need to hear it about six times. Even Jesus had to call some people by their name twice to try to get their attention. How many times does he have to call our name until we listen, trust, and obey?

There are only three times recorded in the Bible where Jesus repeats a person's name twice (not including when he called out God's name while on the cross) and that is when he is making an unusually important statement. It is usually when the person has not been very responsive and needs a good shaking. Have you ever tried getting a point across to someone, and they just didn't get it, or they just wouldn't pay attention? Did you just want to shake them and say, "Wake up" or "Listen"?

The Apostle Peter

Jesus called Peter by name twice when he was being too self-confident and not enough "Jesus-confident." The apostle Peter had to strongly be reminded how much he needed Jesus to survive the attacks of Satan, "*Simon, Simon,* Satan has asked to sift you as wheat. But I have prayed for you, Simon, that your faith may not fail" (Luke 22:31, emphasis mine). Are you trusting in God for strength to stand against the tactics of Satan? Or is Jesus not enough? Do we need New Age techniques or eastern religious practices or new and improved "church" programs to stand strong in our faith?

The Apostle Paul

Another time Jesus called someone by name twice was to a religious leader who wanted to murder and destroy anyone who believed in Jesus as the Christ, the Son of the living God. This man surely had a radical, transforming encounter with Jesus. This religious man was going full-steam ahead with what he thought was pleasing to God. Jesus had to come into his life in a powerful and disturbing way. He said, "*Saul, Saul,* why do you persecute me?" (See Acts 9:1-22, emphasis mine).

Lightning had to strike from heaven to get Saul's attention to stop and listen to Jesus. Saul was brought to his knees and was blinded by the light. Saul's blindness limited his distractions. He finally *listened to* Jesus and obeyed. After his transformation, Saul went on to become the great apostle Paul.

What will it take us to stop, fall to our knees and listen to Jesus—to hear his voice?

Mary and Martha

Jesus also called twice to a believer who was too distracted by her misguided desire, wanting her own way, and wanting to give a good appearance for the Lord. She missed what Jesus wanted, which was to take time out of her busy schedule and sit at his feet and listen to him, in stillness and quietness. This was what her sister was already doing. These two sisters you know as Mary and Martha.

Mary made a conscious decision to sit at Jesus' feet and listen to God's word. Mary's sister Martha did not make that conscious decision to listen to Jesus. Martha let the distraction of the day keep her from enjoying Jesus. Martha was so caught up in getting "things" done that she missed the most important "thing"—to listen to Jesus. Martha's perspective was distorted. Here she thought she was doing something pleasing for Jesus when in reality she was neglecting him. (This is similar to a husband who tries so hard to please his wife with "things" when in reality he neglects her more important emotional needs.) Martha actually felt such self-pity at not having her "sacrifice" recognized that she complained and ordered Jesus to get Mary to help her:

> Lord, *don't you care* that my sister has left me to do the work by myself? *Tell her* to help me! (Luke 10:40, emphasis mine)

Jesus had to stop Martha and tell her what really mattered to him. Jesus replied, "*Martha, Martha*, you are worried and upset about many things, but only *one thing* is needed"(Luke 10:41, emphasis mine).

One Thing

Remember the movie, "City Slickers"? The part that really interested me was when Curly, played by Jack Palance, was telling Billy Crystal about the most important thing in life. Jack Palance held up one finger, and Billy Crystal thought his index finger was the most important thing. By the end of the movie, he realized what Curly meant.

The most important thing in life is that which means the most to you. It is the one thing that you get so involved with to the point of losing yourself. That one thing becomes the focus of your intention and your life. For Billy Crystal, it was saving a cow's life. For that moment, saving the cow was the only thing that mattered, even to the point of risking his own life. What are you willing to risk your life for? What is the one thing in your life that means the most to you?

For what you treasure and value the most, that is where your heart will be. (Matt. 6:21)

Jesus says, Heaven and earth will pass away, but my words will never pass away. (Matt. 24:35)

Jesus is saying that what you focus on will be your desire and passion. "No one can serve two masters" (Matt. 6:24). Jesus demands your total devotion. You can't split your devotion in two. Mary knew the importance of Jesus and his words.

Jesus told Martha, "Only one thing is needed. Mary has chosen what is better, and it will not be taken away from her" (Luke. 10:42). And what is that "one thing" that is needed and that Mary was doing? Was she busy doing important things that needed to be done? Was she helping the sick or ministering to those in need? Was she preoccupied with the cares and distractions of her busy life? No, Mary was just sitting at the feet of Jesus and listening to him. This is the one thing that was needed at that specific moment—to show her love to Jesus by listening to him. Some would say she was being lazy and irresponsible. However, those other needs of showing hospitality, helping the sick, or ministering to the needy were better met at a different time.

Why did Jesus say listening to him was the one thing that was needed? Because everything else for which we strive, achieve, and accomplish will be destroyed, but our relationship with God lasts through eternity.

> Lift up your eyes to the heavens,
> look at the earth beneath;
> the heavens will vanish like smoke,
> the earth will wear out like a garment
> and its inhabitants die like flies.
> But my salvation will last forever,
> my righteousness will never fail. (Isa. 51:6)

We need to take time to lift our eyes to God and away from the present distractions of the world. We need to constantly be recharged and renewed in his presence. All else is temporary in our lives except God, who is eternal.

> Though the mountains be shaken
> and the hills be removed,
> yet my unfailing love for you will not
> be shaken nor my covenant of
> peace be removed, says the
> LORD, who has compassion on you. (Isa. 54.10)

Meditation Helps Our Service

This does not mean we have to join a monastery and spend all our time in meditation on God and his Word (although a visit to one might offer a refreshing time of solitude). We are to be involved with daily chores of life, but hopefully, leaning on God's power and not our own (Zech.4: 6). We can always take the time given to us by God and return a portion of it to him by spending personal time with him. Not just a token prayer, a quick reading of a Bible verse, or the busyness of church life, but a true commitment to the Almighty and a conscious decision to "Be still and know that *he is* God" (Ps. 46:10, emphasis added and modified).

My Monastery Experience

Recently, I went to a monastery in New Mexico to get away from the daily distractions of the busy world and work on this book. Again, it took time to slow down and focus on God in silence and stillness. However, after about a week of solitude, silence, stillness, meditation, prayer, and Bible reading, I was renewed in my relationship and passion with God. When I returned home after a week, I was more energized to glorify God in service to him and others. The quiet time with God was renewing, refreshing, and rewarding.

What will it take for God to bring us to our knees and see him for who he truly is—an almighty, powerful God who loves us unconditionally and wants to transform our life? How many times does God have to call our name? In fact, can you hear him calling you by name now—gently, softly, and lovingly? Jesus is standing at the door of your heart knocking, asking to come in to live with you (Rev. 3:20). He is gently calling your name.

So, do you want to be a Martha or a Mary? The right choice will be honor, glory and praise to God. God wants all of our attention, and he wants us to know him personally, passionately, and powerfully. God wants to transform us into his likeness (2 Cor. 3:18).

Meditate on Jesus. This is one thing that is vital in our relationship with God. Our time we set aside to be quiet and still in the presence of the almighty God will bring us closer to God in a more intimate way.

Therefore, if we focus on God and our personal relationship with him, by spending time with him, then he will become our "Guiding Light", "As the World Turns" and "All the Days of Our Lives". The "Dark Shadows" will vanish, and we will no longer be like the "Young and the Restless".

Practical Applications

Mentally, Physically, Emotionally, Spiritually

Here are some *practical physical tips* on how to slow down, be still, and know God. Some of these tips can be combined or done singularly. The main thing is to find which method(s) help you to slow down to focus on God and feel his ever-loving presence. This will transform you and increase your intimacy with God.

The Mary Factor

Follow the *Mary Factor (Luke 10:39)*: Mary *sat* at *Jesus' feet*, a *position of submission, attentiveness and focus*. She *mentally* decided to listen, *physically* prepared herself to sit at Jesus' feet, which then prepared her *spiritually* to receive God's Word.

Mentally

1. *Make a decision* that you will block out time in your schedule to be still and *meditate* on God.
2. *Schedule a time.* It won't happen on its own. I schedule the time in my appointment book to

have quiet time with God.

3. *Give yourself permission* to use this time as God has designed you to take a rest in him. You're not goofing off; you are obeying God and drawing near to him. You are being renewed by his presence.

4. You might say, *"I don't have time."* Well, you don't have time not to. People who have heart attacks end up finding the time for rest and stillness. *Jesus only had three years to complete his mission of saving the world*, and he knew he didn't have time *not* to continually go to his Father in prayer, solitude, and meditation.

5. *Mentally prepare yourself.* Read the Scriptures of how God wants us to be still and know him. Read the passages of Jesus getting away to be alone with God and how he tells us to find rest with him. (See pages 41 to 42 and 118 to 121).

6. As you meditate, *whenever other thoughts come into your mind*, simply say to yourself, "I don't have to think about this now" and let the thought float away. Go back to the relaxing scene, Scripture, phrase, or word on which you are focusing. Remember, you can meditate on God's word, works, and wonders.

Physically

1. *Find a quiet, restful place* with subdued lighting if possible to *meditate* on God and his word, works, and wonders. Leave the house; get away from the kids.

2. *Take deep, slow, belly breaths* and slowly exhale.

3. *You can practice various physical postures* that might help you enter into greater reverence and intimacy with God. We find various postures

throughout the Bible that people have used to show respect and honor to God. See which ones help you to be still and know God better.

- *Standing* (1 Kings 8:22; Matt. 6:5; Mark 11:25; Luke 18:11).
- *Kneeling* (1 Kings 8:54; 2 Chron. 6:13; Ezra 9:5; Dan. 6:10; Acts 7:60; 9:40; 20:36; 21:5).
- *Bowing* (Gen. 24:26; Exod.11:8; 12:27-28; Ps. 95:6; Isa. 45:23; Eph. 3:14).
- *Prostration* (to lie down flat on your stomach and face) (Gen. 17:3; Num. 14:5; 16:4, 45; 20:6; 1 Kings 18:42; Job 1:20; Mark 5:22; John 11:32).

> Then he returned to his disciples and found them sleeping. "Could you men not keep watch with me for one hour?" he asked Peter. "Watch and pray so that you will not fall into temptation. The spirit is willing, but the body is weak." (Matt 26:40-41)

- *Sit down* with your back straight but not stiff. This helps you to stay awake.

4. *Close your eyes* and let your body rest with un-crossed arms and legs. You can visualize or feel the presence of God with you. There is Jesus right with you.
5. *Focus your attention on your hands and arms.* Let them get very heavy, then let your feet and legs get heavy.
6. *Picture each part of your body becoming re-laxed, see the muscles going loose and limp and then feel heaviness develop, feel stress being re-leased.* Allow your body to sink into the support

of where you are relaxing.

7. *Feel God's warm caring presence fill* your body with his peace and love.

8. *Tune in to your natural breathing, heartbeat, and pulse.* Just go with the flow of your natural rhythm. Allowing God to take over and fill you with his presence and peace which he promises.

9. *You can also be outside in* nature and reflect on the beauty of God's creation. For example, you can take a nature walk and discover God's beautiful works and wonders all around you. You can also assume a still position as reviewed above, and focus on one of your senses, such as listening to the forest sounds or smelling the ocean air. You will surely be meditating on God's works and wonders!

Emotionally and Spiritually

1. *Prepare to start off with spending 5 minutes in silence with God*; gradually increase to twenty minutes and at times one hour.

2. *Think of God* and his care and love for you.

3. *Let your mind wander* to a favorite place, image, or restful idea. Pretend you are going on a vacation, taking a hike through the mountains or the meadows of God's creation. Imagine the warm, gentle hands of God holding you. Find an image that is peaceful, safe, and comforting for you *to meditate* on while giving glory to God. — discover God's works.

4. *Review real-life experiences* that are comforting and give praise to God. What do you have to be thankful for? *Meditate* on these things, —part of God's wonders.

5. *Listen to soothing music* to still your soul.

These are practical suggestions that help facilitate being still in the presence of God. Discover what works for you, and practice daily meditative times with God to become intimate with him. God will transform your life (2 Cor. 3:18).

Let's now learn from some other people of God and see how they came to know (love) and hear God on an intimate level, and ultimately how that led to their renewal, revival, and transformation.

III

From the Mountaintop to the Rooftop

5

A Mountaintop Experience

My Mountaintop Experience

I remember when I was a young boy and would visit my aunt and uncle in upstate New York. They lived in the country and had mountains in their backyard. I always dreamed of climbing those mountains to see what was on the other side. However, it was almost impossible to reach even the base of the mountains, because the land in front of the mountains consisted of acres of deep swamps. Every summer, I dreamed about climbing these mountains. Finally, one year I decided to try. I was about ten years old. I did not tell anyone where I was going because they would not have allowed me to go. They would consider it too dangerous.

I found some wood planks and took them with me to walk across the swamps. Finally, I made it to the base of the mountain and was ready to climb to the top!

The terrain was dense forest. It was shaded and cool and not much sunlight came through. I climbed and climbed—wondering if I was ever going to make it to the top.

I finally reached the top of the mountain, something I had dreamed about for years. To my surprise it was nothing like I expected. I thought I would see another town on the other side. What I saw instead was truly breathtaking.

The other side of the mountain did not slope down but rather extended out into rolling plains. Sunshine lit up the entire landscape. It was a tremendous contrast to the dark, cool, dense forest. There were all different shades of green, yellow, red, and orange. The rolling hills extended for miles. You could smell the fresh grass and flowers. The birds were flying gracefully. It was like I had entered into another world; I felt like Alice in Wonderland. It was beautiful and peaceful. It felt like heaven to me. I just stood in silence and in awe. I did not want to go back into the dark, cold, damp forest. I just wanted to stay and enjoy the sunshine and beautiful view. However, I knew my mother would be calling me soon to eat dinner. So, reluctantly I returned home, knowing I would always treasure the experience in my heart.

But my experience, no matter how majestic and glorious, does not hold a candle to what Peter, James, and John experienced on the Mount of Transfiguration in Matthew 17. Although my vision seemed glorious to me, they experienced the glory of Heaven.

Peter's Mountaintop Experience

I cannot know how it must have felt for Peter, James, and John as they watched Jesus transform before their very eyes on what is now called the Mount of Transfiguration (Matthew 17). Imagine yourself standing there watching Jesus' appearance change right before your eyes (Matt. 17:2 MSG).

You see a light as bright as the sun shining through his face. His clothes fill with a bright white light that radiates outward like rays of sunshine. The light coming from Jesus is so bright, it is almost blinding. You have to cover your eyes as you try to figure out what is going on. And then you see Moses and Elijah there, talking with Jesus.

What kind of reaction or response would you have? Would you stand in awe with your mouth hanging open?

Speechless? I can imagine James and John reacting like that, but not Peter; he had a problem being silent and still. He wanted to talk about building shelters for the three glowing figures! Basically, God had to shut Peter up and tell him to listen. "Will you just listen and stop babbling!" (Matt. 17:5 MSG). God had to come down in a bright cloud, envelop them and say, "This is my Son, whom I love; with him I am well pleased. Listen to him!" (Matt. 17:5). If we don't babble with our mouths, we still might have much babbling in our heads. Are we ever like Peter? Does God ever have to grab our attention, even when we are surrounded by his glory, so we listen to him?

Peter's Rooftop Experience

Peter went from the mountaintop experience to a rooftop experience. He went from the mountaintop with Jesus, Moses, and Elijah, where he met with great difficulty in being still and silent, to the rooftop of Simon the Tanner. Here Peter could pray with a much more listening heart.

Approximately ten years later, the Scriptures describe Peter spending time with God on a rooftop. He seems to have gotten into the practice of having some quiet time with God. The Scriptures say that while Peter was on the roof praying, "he fell into a trance" (Acts 10:10). It was during this focused, meditative, trance-like state that God spoke to Peter and revealed a vision to him (Acts 10:11-13). There are times when I am meditating on God and praying that I feel such a peace and lightness. The experience is similar to being in a trance where my attention is focused on God and nothing else. What a wonderful, blissful experience with God!

This experience of Peter meditating on God resulted in another transformation in Peter's life. Peter realized he was being prejudiced, and so he repented. We see that even the apostle Peter needed to be transformed. It is during these quiet times with God (when we focus on him and clear our minds of distracting thoughts) that we are most receptive to hearing God's Word.

To this day, you can visit houses like that of Simon the Tanner in Joppa, Israel. It was the custom for Eastern houses to have flat roofs, which were convenient for privacy and relaxation. I was able to visit Simon the Tanner's house several years ago and sit on the roof, overlooking the Mediterranean Sea, and meditate like Peter. It was an awesome and renewing experience.

My Rooftop Experience

I used to have rooftop experiences on a regular basis with the Lord in solitude and prayer. Twenty years ago, I lived in Albuquerque, New Mexico. The houses and buildings in Albuquerque have flat roofs like those in Joppa, Israel. At that time I lived at the Christian student center where people would come and go. The center had a section of flat roof. So, guess where I went to be alone with God? I would climb up the side of the wall and go on the rooftop to be alone with God to pray and meditate with him. While it was wonderful to imitate the physical surroundings of Peter, that is not always practical. Instead, we must imitate the spiritual surroundings in our hearts.

Practical Applications

No matter where I live or visit, I always try to find a place of solitude, away from the crowds and busyness, to refocus my thoughts and heart on God. Even at work, I take breaks and try to go places where no one can find me. Otherwise, I am easily distracted, drained, and discouraged. I asked a class

I was teaching about this subject, "How can you have moments of solitude with God?" Here are some of their answers:

A young mother with two active children and a busy life said, "I go into the bathroom and lock the door to get away and pray."

One man said, "I get up at 4:00 or 5:00 in the morning when things are more quiet and peaceful and sit in silence and stillness before the Lord."

Another man said, "I take a walk in the woods and praise God for his beautiful creations."

Another woman said, "I just stare at the sunset and give God the glory."

The one place of solitude I can usually depend on no matter where I am, whether at college, work, a social gathering is the *restroom*. It is a place where I can be alone from the crowds and be in solitude. Maybe that's why they call it a *rest* room.

I also try to meditate daily for twenty minutes while listening to a tape I made on being still with Jesus. I turn off the phone ringer and relax in his love.

Where can you go to be alone, away from people, phones, and faxes?

Where can you have a rooftop experience?

6

Moses Meets God
Face to Face

The Challenge

Moses says to God, "Now show me your glory"
(Exod. 33:18). "Show me what you've got! Show
me what you're made of!" Being from New York
and growing up with gangs, fights, drugs, and other violent
things, I think of these statements as fighting words. When
you face your challengers and want to see if they are bluff-
ing, you tell them to reveal themselves.

However, Moses is not picking a fight with God when he
says to God, "Now show me your glory" (Exod. 33:18).
Moses was tired and discouraged. He had a heavy burden
leading the Israelites to the Promised Land. The thousands of
Israelites were pressuring him and continually complaining.
The surrounding nations were against the Israelite nation.
Moses needed some reassurance from God that he was going
to be with Moses and carry out his mighty promises. He ex-
pressed his concern and worries to God and asked some
questions. God's answer was, "My presence will go with
you, and I will give you rest" (Exod. 33:14).

Sometimes God's promises are not according to our time-
table, so we doubt and become frustrated. Do you know any-

one who is a big talker? You know the kind—always making grandiose promises but seldom living up to them. You grow tired and weary of their empty promises. You begin to doubt their integrity. However, this is not so with God. We see throughout the Scriptures that he fulfills his promises.

Even though Moses was growing impatient, God agreed to show some of his glory and power. This was going to happen on the mountaintop of Mount Sinai. However, it was close to 1,400 years later when Moses saw the long awaited promise of Jesus' heavenly glory on earth. Moses again witnessed God's glory, along with Elijah, when they were with Jesus on the Mount of Transfiguration. Sometimes the best things in life are worth waiting for.

I had the awesome experience, a couple of times, of climbing Mount Sinai in Egypt and seeing God's glory. A group of us were given instructions to be ready in the morning to go up on Mount Sinai. We met at the base of the mountain around 1:30 A.M. ready for a three-hour hike because we wanted to get to the top to watch the sunrise. Once we reached the top, we sat and waited to see God reveal his glory. The view was breathtaking. God *is* awesome. He continually reveals his glory all around us. However, we need to be in tune with God to notice it and appreciate it.

Moses is Called to Be Holy

Moses was called by God to get ready to meet the Great I Am (Exod. 34:2) on top of Mount Sinai. In order to truly experience God, we need to prepare ourselves to meet him, to see him, and to hear him. God requires holiness from us. God had Moses separate himself from the other people. "Present yourself to me there on top of the mountain. No one is to come with you or be seen anywhere on the mountain" (Exod. 34:2-3).

Moses had learned about his need to sometimes separate himself from the people to meet with God alone. When Moses wanted to meet with God and hear his wisdom, he went to the tent he put up outside the camp, in other words, to be away from the people (Exod. 33:7). This was where he met with God in privacy and solitude. The Lord spoke to Moses face to face, as a person would speak to a friend (Exod. 33:11). Moses found rest and security in God's presence. Jesus' words ring out:

> Come to me, all you who are weary and burdened, and I will give you rest. Take my yoke upon you and learn from me, for I am gentle and humble in heart, and you will find rest for your souls. For my yoke is easy and my burden is light. (Matt. 11:28)

God Meets His Challenge

God showed his glory to Moses. When Moses came down from Mount Sinai, his face was radiant, because he had been with God (Exod. 34:29). Does being in the presence of God, while allowing him to work through us, produce a noticeable change in our appearance? What type of radiance was this coming from Moses' face? Was it a glowing brightness like the sun? Can we be radiant with the glow of the Son within us? Yes!

Moses was affected by his personal encounter with God. However, he continually needed to spend close, intimate time with God to recharge the glow. The glowing face of Moses would fade as he was away from the Lord (2 Cor. 3:13; Exod. 34:29; 34:33-35).

How did Moses get a recharge and revival of the Lord's powerful radiance? Moses went to the Lord in solitude and prayer (Exod. 34:33, 35). When Moses came into the presence of Almighty God, he was transformed. This is how God recharged him. Moses had an intimate relationship with God. However, he had to *continually* come into God's holy and transforming presence.

God Does the Transforming

This experience with Moses was so powerful that the apostle Paul later refers to this event. Paul, who experienced a brilliant light from Jesus (Acts 9:3), makes reference to the fading radiance of Moses' face and how one can now reflect God's glory. Paul reveals how we can be transformed into the likeness of God, from whom this transformation comes.

And we, who with unveiled faces all reflect the Lord's glory, are being transformed into his likeness with the ever-increasing glory, which comes from the Lord, who is the Spirit. (2 Cor. 3:18)

People have tried throughout thousands of years to be transformed by going to extreme measures of asceticism, putting their bodies through suffering, performing numerous religious practices, trying new methods and techniques, and adding new programs to their church. We are so familiar with the concept that we think that we have to have certain techniques or that we have to perform really well to achieve great things.

We can do as many religious things as we want, but it will not cause or effect our transformation into the likeness of God. That is because it comes from God's powerful Holy Spirit (2 Cor. 3:18). It is like trying to shine a flashlight into the sun to make it brighter. There is no comparison between the two lights and sources of power.

We can compare the process to getting a suntan. It is the *sun's power* that transforms the color of our skin. The more time we spend in the sun, the darker our bodies become.

However, the sun can only tan the skin we expose. Likewise, if we want to experience the living and powerful Holy God, and be transformed into his likeness and radiate with his glow, we need to come into his presence and learn to be still and silent. This is a process, and it takes time.

It Takes Practice, But There is a Reward!

We need to practice being still in his presence. It takes time to learn how to silence all the distractions and noises in our mind and body. Moses spent 40 days and 40 nights with God on a high, desolate mountain in solitude, stillness, and fasting (Exod. 34:28).

I know in my own experiences that it takes time to be still and to quiet my soul to be more in tune to God. This spiritual discipline of training ourselves to stop and slow down before God is very healing in many ways—emotionally, physically, and spiritually. However, some things get worse before they get better. It's like when I clean my fish tank. The dirt gets stirred up, making the tank look worse than before I started cleaning it. Eventually more of the stirred-up dirt is removed, and the tank becomes cleaner than before.

Transformation is not always pleasant. God's messages often produce uncomfortable feelings, emotions, and thoughts. For example, God may convict us of sin that requires our repentance. Repentance involves change, and we are not always comfortable with change, but if we allow God to change us, we will be healed and forgiven.

People tend to follow their natural instincts to run away from pain and to run to comfort. We don't like to face physical, emotional, or spiritual issues that are painful. Instead, we become addicted to distractions and means of escape, such as alcohol, drugs, sex, shopping, work, food, the Internet, and TV. Only God can truly heal us and forgive us of our sins.

God will forgive us, restore us, heal us, save us, and transform us if we come to him with humble hearts, in prayer and repentance. God says:

> If my people, who are called by my name, will humble themselves and pray and seek my face and turn from their wicked ways, then will I hear from heaven and will forgive their sin and will heal their land. (2 Chron. 7:14)

Wouldn't it be great to be able to have that same kind of relationship as God had with Moses? How wonderful it would be to speak to God, "face to face, as a man speaks with his friend" (Exod. 33:11).

My Maysville Experience

I remember a time I wanted to spend more time with God and draw closer to him through meditation and solitude. I retreated from the busyness of civilization and camped out in the woods by a lake. That experience helped me know God on a much deeper level.

I went to Maysville, North Carolina. It was a quiet, secluded place. There were no phones, faxes, or e-mails to distract me. I set up my tent under the trees by a stream. A short distance away was a beautiful lake with no one around. I started to fast.

Even in such a peaceful setting, it took me about a week to become still and feel the presence, power, and the glory of God. Initially, it was hard focusing on nothing but God. I was easily distracted. It takes much practice to be still. This experience showed me the need to practice more quiet time on a regular basis to clear my mind of all the clutter and insignificant things. However, this solitary time with God made me long even more to just sit at the feet of Jesus, to be still and silent, so that I could hear and feel God's presence.

As the deer pants for the stream of water, so my soul pants for you, O God. My soul thirsts for God, for the living God. When can I go and meet with God? (Ps. 42:1)

We quench and grieve the Spirit of God with all our worldly distractions and noises that often lead to sin. Sometimes we expect God to show us a sign as he did at the time of the prophets, with fire from heaven. However, back then, as now, God speaks to us in the gentle stillness of our hearts, with a whisper, convicting us by his word. Remember the other prophet with Jesus on the Mount of Transfiguration? He was Elijah. God spoke to him in a gentle whisper. Elijah also had a mountaintop experience with God.

In the next chapter we will look at how Elijah had intimacy with God and how he was transformed.

7

Elijah Hears
the Gentle Whisper

Have you ever felt so depressed and discouraged that you just wanted to die? Have you ever felt lonely, tired, or fearful? Have you ever wondered what's the use of living? Have you ever prayed and asked God to take your life? Have you ever felt completely worn out and dried up? Have you ever felt like you are the only one with your concerns and problems? If so, you should be able to relate to the great Prophet of God, Elijah, who was with Moses and Jesus on the Mount of Transfiguration (Matt. 17).

Elijah was the chief of God's prophets. Elijah was the one to prepare the way of the Lord (Mal. 4:5-6; Matt. 17: 9-13; Mark 9:12-13). To this day, when the Jewish people celebrate the Passover meal, they leave an empty plate and chair for Elijah to come to prepare the way for their Messiah. Of course, this has already been fulfilled. Elijah did come and so did the Messiah, Jesus Christ (Matt. 17: 11-12; Mark 9:12-13).

As with Moses and Jesus, Elijah had a mountaintop experience when God revealed his power.

His mountain was Mount Carmel, where he had victory over the 450 prophets of Baal. (See 1 Kings 18.) Elijah was confronted by his challenger Ahab (v.17). Elijah was defending the true God of Israel, while Ahab was defending the pagan god, Baal. Elijah challenged the people of Israel to make a choice and stop dancing around between the true God of Israel and Baal (v. 21). Elijah challenged the 450 prophets of their god, Baal, to "duke it out" with the true God (v. 22-39). The God of Israel won by revealing himself with fire from heaven (v. 38). "When the people saw this, they fell prostrate and cried, 'The LORD—he is God! The LORD—he is God!'" (v. 39). Then Elijah had the 450 prophets of Baal slaughtered (v. 40). Elijah was victorious through the power of God.

After this experience, Elijah received a threat on his life that scared him. He fled for his life (1 Kings 19:3). He, like Moses and Jesus, spent forty nights in solitude without food (1 Kings 19:8). Elijah finally reached the mountain of God, which is believed to be Mount Sinai. Elijah felt discouraged, fearful, and depressed. He became depressed to the point of wanting to die (1 Kings 19:4).

Elijah was stripped emotionally, physically, and spiritually. It is during these times in our lives, times of great weaknesses, in which we tend to allow God to work through us most. We are more able to rely on God's grace for our strength through our weaknesses. God told the suffering apostle Paul, "My grace is sufficient for you for my power is made perfect in weakness" (2 Cor. 12:9).

Hard times can also produce greater intimacy with God, but first we must strip off all our false layers, such as pride and self-reliance. How do we strip down? We strip down by falling empty handed on our knees before God. We can also strip off false layers by fasting and by having solitude with God. We need to become weak in ourselves before God can work his power through us and we can receive his glory.

My Desert Experience

One summer, I went on a desert survival course for fourteen days. This trip reminded me of Elijah, Moses and Jesus in the desert. My desert experience stripped me down physically and emotionally. During the first three days of the survival course, we were given no food, water, or supplies. We were totally reliant on the things we could find along the way while hiking in the Utah desert in 100-degree temperatures. We hiked up and down mountains, cliffs, and valleys. We experienced elevations between 6,000 and 10,000 feet above sea level. We soon became weak, thirsty, hungry, and exhausted. I was ready to quit after the first two days and wanted to every day after that. We had no matches, watches, flashlights, sleeping bags, tents, razors, or toilets. We had to survive off the land and we hiked ten to twenty miles a day.

My sufferings on this trip helped me to depend on God in a much greater way. It was a trying experience, but I used the time to draw closer to God in a more personal and intimate way.

The Solo Experience

This trip included three solo days that each of us spent alone in the desert. I spent these three days without food. I used this solo time with God to meditate on him, to pray, and to listen to him speak to me through his word and through the beauty of his creation. I also used this time to write some of this book.

I built a shelter for myself out of tree branches, leaves, and bark. I needed it to stay warm and dry because it rained much of the time. My shelter looked like a rib cage of a big animal in which I was trapped because of the harsh weather conditions.

Moments of Discouragement

Throughout the desert experience, I kept hoping for an earth-shattering experience with God. I expected him to reveal himself to me in some mighty way while I was alone in the desert, starving and meditating on him. This thought especially occurred while I was on my solo experience. Instead, it rained, and I got cold at night and was miserable. Where was God? Why wasn't he revealing himself? I faced moments of doubt and discouragement.

A Revelation

And then it happened! As I was looking out of my little wooden rib-cage shelter, I remembered the story of Jonah in the belly of a great fish for three days. I also reflected on Jesus being in the dark and dreary belly of the earth for three days. I was reminded how it must have felt for Moses, Elijah, and Jesus in their quiet, still moments in the desert. God began convicting my heart in the dark, quiet moments of my solitude. I began to remember many of his words from what I read in the Bible.

The hour has come for the Son of Man to be glorified. I tell you the truth, unless a kernel of wheat falls to the ground and dies, it remains only a single seed. But if it dies, it produces many seeds. (John 12:23-24)

During my desert experience, God was telling me through his word and convicting me in my heart that I must give my life fully over to him and not rely on my own strength and abilities. I certainly had a lot less strength and abilities during my desert experience. I could hardly even start a fire. In truth, it took me ten days to learn how to build a fire without matches. About the same time I concluded that I would burn up more calories trying to start the fire than were in the food I had to eat.

Moments of Encouragement

I was also encouraged to realize what happened after the experiences of Moses, Elijah, Jonah, Jesus, and others after their solo experiences with God. Moses came down the mountain with the law of God. Elijah went on to prepare the way of the Lord. Jonah reluctantly preached eight words to the Ninevites (Jonah 3:4) and more than 120,000 people turned to God and were saved. Jesus conquered death and rose from the grave to give us an eternal hope with victory over death.

I knew God had a plan for me if I would just trust and obey him. I learned to rely on him. I developed a deeper, closer, and more personal relationship with God. I was transformed! However, first I had to be stripped down and silenced.

Because of this experience, I can relate to Elijah when he was going through his own survival course in 1 Kings 19. God puts us through different types of "survival courses" throughout our life so that we can learn to trust and rely on him who is sovereign.

Elijah withdrew into a cave. Did you ever feel like hiding in a cave where no one could find you, or have you felt as if you were in a dark cave and nobody cared about you?

Well, God does care. God came to Elijah and told him to "go out and stand on the mountain in the presence of the Lord, for the Lord is about to pass by" (1 Kings 19:3-11). What did Elijah expect when God said this? The Lord just told Elijah that he was going to do a "fly by." Satan tries to deceive us into believing that if there is not a really big show, then it is boring and unfulfilling. Satan continually tries to seduce us with all his fancy glitter, which is empty and destructive.

I could imagine Elijah just waiting for some big, powerful, earth-shattering show to be performed by God—perhaps similar to an air show.

Have you ever been to one? Perhaps, you waited for the Stealth—the fastest, loudest, most sophisticated and most powerful plane to do a fly by. You experience various things when it flies past you. You hear the loud noises as it breaks the sound barrier. You feel the ground shake. You duck and cover your ears and face. You feel a powerful rumbling.

Elijah Meets God

Well, Elijah was waiting for the great and powerful Lord to "pass by" (1 Kings 19:11). Then suddenly "a great and powerful wind tore the mountain apart and shattered the rocks... but the Lord was not in the wind. After the wind, there was an earthquake... but the Lord was not in the earthquake. After the earthquake came a fire... but the Lord was not in the fire. And after the fire came a *gentle whisper*." When Elijah heard it, he pulled his cloak over his face and went out and stood at the mouth of the cave (1 Kings 19:12-13, emphasis mine). And God spoke to Elijah and gave him his mission and renewed his faith.

Do you need God to renew and refocus your heart, mind, body, and soul on his mission and renew and strengthen your faith? Will it come from a new man-made church program? Will it come from a powerful, earth-shattering seminar or workshop? Or will it come from standing still and quiet in his presence so that he can transform you?

Trusting in God

I want to hear the still, gentle whisper of God calling me, reassuring me to trust in him and to know that he is God, that he is in control and everything will be all right. But now I know that for me to hear God, I need to be still and wait patiently for him. "Be still before the LORD and wait patiently for him" (Ps. 37:7).

My problem is that I often want to be in control of things. These feelings arise when I don't trust in who God is. Also, many times we try to numb our pain or hide the hurt with noise or distraction. We add more things, gadgets, toys, and responsibilities to our lives for fulfillment. We try desperately to take control over our own lives. Yet the more we do that, the more we actually lose control and even blame it on God, or we wonder why God isn't helping us. Our dreams become shattered and broken because we did not trust and wait patiently for the Lord.

Broken Dreams

As children bring their broken toys
With tears for us to mend,
I brought my broken dreams to God
Because he is my friend.
But then instead of leaving him
In peace to work alone,
I hung around and tried to help
With many that were my own.
At last, I snatched them back and cried,
"How could you be so slow?"
"My child," He said, "What could I do?"
"You never did let go."

Author unknown

Letting go involves trust. Trust involves knowing the person well enough to trust him or her, just as a child who jumps off a high bunk bed into the hands of his loving father knows that his father will catch him and not let him fall.

How do we get to know someone well enough to trust him or her with our lives? How do we get to know God enough to start trusting him with our entire life?

God gives the answer. "Be still and know that I am God" (Ps. 46:10). We need to come into his presence in solitude, in quietness, and in prayer, meditatively listening to him speaking to our hearts.

Are you open to hearing God now in his gentle whisper? Are you willing to follow the advice Eli gave young Samuel? Eli said, "Go lie down and say, 'Speak LORD, for your servant is listening'" (1 Sam. 3:9). Samuel at first thought it was Eli calling him. Samuel was obedient in responding to Eli several times in a row, until Eli figured out that it was God calling Samuel. He already had a spirit willing to serve and listen, and that was probably why God chose to speak to him. It was surely a gentle whisper that God used, since Samuel after all thought it was Eli! We need to find a quiet place of solitude and meditate silently, while asking God to speak to us because we are listening.

Practical Application

Find a quiet place to sit down away from noises and distractions. Focus on the presence of God in your midst. You can keep your eyes open or closed. You can stare out the window or stare out into space in the room. Some like to stare at a candle flame to relax. Try not to ask God anything. Just sit quietly and still. Meditate on God filling the room with his presence. Appreciate his gentle touch, and allow him in this silence and stillness to renew and restore you. Know in your deepest heart how much he unconditionally loves you. Don't have any predetermined expectations of what will happen.

Just enjoy your time together with
God in your room.

Do this for five to twenty minutes.

8

Jesus Hears His
Father's Voice

The late Dr. W. B. West was an inspiration to me. He was a pioneer in the formation of graduate school training in theology and a great biblical scholar. Dr. West would travel throughout the country to recruit people for graduate training in the Bible. He commented on how often people would cite a lack of time as a reason for not going to graduate school. These people were usually already involved in the ministry.

Dr. West would respond by telling them a story about a man mowing his lawn with a dull blade. The mower would continually get clogged up because the dull blade would not cut the grass efficiently anymore. The man had to go over sections of grass constantly because the blade would not always cut the first time through. This man's neighbor noticed the problem and suggested that the man take time out to sharpen his mower blade. The man said he did not have time to sharpen the blade, because he had a lot of grass to finish cutting. In the end, it took him much longer, with much greater difficulty, to cut the grass.

We tend to be under the same delusion that we do not have time to stop and sharpen our blades. We have an important task or project we have to finish. We have a lot of work to do. How would we have time to stop and get refreshed and renewed? The answer is found in our Master Teacher.

Jesus Took Time to be Still

I do not think any of us have more important work to do than Jesus did when he began his ministry. Dr. Luke says Jesus was about thirty years old when he began his ministry (Luke 3:23). Jesus knew why he came into the world, which was to seek and save the lost (Luke 19:10). He only had about three years to complete his mission. What was the first thing Jesus did when he began his ministry after being baptized? He went into the desert of solitude for forty days without food (Matt. 4:1-11; Mark 1:12-13; Luke 4:1-13). How could Jesus do this? Didn't he know he didn't have much time to work? Didn't he know that salvation for the entire world depended upon him?

Jesus knew exactly what he was doing. He knew the need to follow God's Spirit wherever he led Jesus. God the Father wanted Jesus to go through the desert of solitude for two main reasons: first, Jesus set the example for all followers of God by spending time in solitude with God before he acted. He *needed* this prayerful time. Second, he demonstrated how every child of God could overcome temptation by depending on God, even when very physically weak. Jesus was tempted in *every* way, just like us (Heb. 2:15, 4:15-16). Where does our strength and power come from? Where else but God, our creator! Moreover, what better way to go to him in solitude and prayer as Jesus often did?

The Desert Trio

We see Moses, Elijah, and Jesus all spending forty days in

the wilderness of solitude and fasting, being tested and tried. Their relationship with God, the Father, was enhanced through this desert experience. Going through such a desert experience reveals of what we are really made. We are all made of the same material as the human Christ. Going through a desert experience *with* God gives us a chance to see that we can rely on God's power, not our own, and that we can achieve more than we ever imaged. But it's up to each one of us to be open to rely on God's strength.

Moses reminds the Israelites how "the LORD your God led you all the way in the desert these forty years, to humble you and test you in order to know what was in your heart, whether or not you would keep his commands" (Deut. 8:1-5). Jesus quotes from this section of Scripture when he was in the desert and Satan tempted him to turn some stones into a loaf of bread. Jesus replies, "It is written: 'Man does not live on bread alone, but on every word that comes from the mouth of God" (Matt. 4:4; Deut. 8:3). Jesus relied on the Word of God and trusted in God for his strength. What was in Jesus' heart was clearly revealed through his desert experience—to obey his Father in heaven. Jesus was able to endure temptations and not give in because his mind was focused on God and his mission.

Continual Renewal

Jesus teaches us the need to have quiet, personal time with God. First he teaches us through his forty-day desert experience, and then he teaches us through his daily quiet times with prayer to God. Jesus continually depended on his Father and was obedient to the Father's will. "I tell you the truth, the Son can do nothing by himself (he realized he could not be self-reliant); he can do only what he sees his Father doing, because whatever the Father does the Son also does" (John

5:19, added comment mine). Do we ever stop to envision God in our place, handling our problems?

Other Scriptures attest to this continual reliance on God:

> Your attitude should be the same as that of Christ Jesus: Who, being in very nature God, did not consider equality with God something to be grasped, but made himself nothing, taking the very nature of a servant, being made in human likeness. And being found in appearance as a man, he humbled himself and became obedient to death—even death on a cross! Therefore God exalted him to the highest place and gave him the name that is above every name, that at the name of Jesus every knee should bow, in heaven and on earth and under the earth, and every tongue confess that Jesus Christ is Lord, to the glory of God the Father. (Phil. 2:5-11)

It is written in Hebrews: "During the days of Jesus' life on earth, he offered up prayers and petitions with loud cries and tears to the one who could save him from death, and he was heard because of his reverent submission" (Heb. 5:7). How often do we pray with loud cries or tears?

Jesus Withdrew From the Crowds

Jesus made it a habit to spend time getting away from all the distractions of the crowds and the world to go to his Father in prayer. Jesus needed to be renewed, refreshed, rejuvenated, and refocused. How often do we decide to go to the movies to renew our energy? How often do we decide to play golf to rejuvenate? Jesus knew that the best way was to be solitary in his heart with God his Father continually.

Very early in the morning, while it was still dark, Jesus got up, left the house and went off to a solitary place, where he prayed. (Mark 1:35)

And after he had dismissed the crowds, he went up on the mountain by himself to pray. When evening came, he was there alone. (Matt. 14:23 RSV)

If Jesus needed to do this, how much more do we need to do it?

Even the apostles had a hard time following Jesus' example. They were teaching and doing great things and did not even have a chance to eat. Jesus said to them, "Come with me by yourselves to a quiet place and get some rest" (Mark 6:31).

If you were an apostle, would your response have gone something like this?

"What do you mean, Jesus? We have so much work to do! Look at all these people who have to be taught God's Word! Look at all these people who need healing! Look at all these lost souls who need to be saved! How can we possibly find a quiet place and rest? We don't have time for that! Let's just work until we knock ourselves out with a heart attack!" This is the excuse most often cited for not having quiet time with Jesus: "I don't have the time." However, in actuality, if we took time out to be refreshed and renewed by God, we would have more energy to be more efficient and productive in doing more work for God.

Having a Healthy Relationship with God

I am reminded of James Dobson, a psychologist of the Christian faith who has many worldwide ministries for Jesus. Several years ago he had a stroke, and he talks now about how that has changed his life. He realized that he required more quiet time with the Lord.

As the wise prophet Isaiah wrote,

> Even youths grow tired and weary, and young men stumble and fall; but those who hope, (or "wait," KJV) in the LORD will renew their strength. They will soar on wings like eagles; they will run and not grow weary, they will walk and not be faint. (Isa. 40:30-31)

The key here is to *hope* or *wait* on the LORD for his renewing power and strength to transform us. King David says, "Be still before the LORD and wait patiently for him" (Ps. 37:7). This takes practice. It is a spiritual discipline to be still before God.

Zechariah says, "Be still before the LORD all mankind" (Zech. 2:13). The prophet Zephaniah says, "Be silent before the Sovereign LORD, for the day of the LORD is near" (Zeph. 1:7).

Jesus knew his time was short for his ministry. He knew the need to keep his focus and strength, which came from God, his Father. We do not know when our life might come to an end, yet we keep waiting for a calmer period in our life to take time out with God. We must prioritize this gentle, intimate time. Jesus already gave us the example. Even with the salvation of the world on his shoulders, he took time to be alone with God. He continually sharpened his "lawnmower blade."

Reading, writing, talking, preparing Bible lessons and sermons, or doing anything else does not take the place of being still and silent before God. We must stop all activities—even Christian activities—and be silent, and simply listen once in a while. Therefore, we can focus and be refreshed by Jesus.

Remember it is not the "earthquake," "fire," or the "trans-figuration" that is renewing, but it is hearing God's "whisper" of love and intimacy that transforms our souls. Does a wife want her husband to hurry through his sweet whispers to her so she can get back to the laundry? Of course not. Those sweet whispers are part of what meets her deepest needs in her marriage. That is our same goal and purpose for having quiet time with God. No other relationship will fulfill our deepest needs, the needs that no spouse can ever fully meet.

The question is not *if* you have time to give to the Lord in stillness and silence, but *do* you have time not to? The next three chapters will focus on practical ways to be still before the Lord—physically, emotionally, and spiritually.

Practical Applications

Find a solitary place where you can be alone with Jesus. Get away from the people, phones, and faxes. Focus on being alone with God. Take a deep breath. Recognize God as the Creator of time. All time belongs to him. Allow him to restore your energy and focus. Allow him to guide your steps into his mission. God will bless the short time you have on this earth, if you give it to him.

Many things seem urgent to us at the moment. We are anxious to get to our business and get things done. We feel we can't take time out to go to God and rest in his loving, renewing presence.

One of my editors who is a teacher wrote the following: "Bill often asks me when I'm still grading papers and reading my textbook around 12:30 A.M., 'Chris Ann, is that crucial for you to have that done by first period tomorrow? Can you stop so you can get some sleep, and be better rested?' And often I can. I lose track of how worthless I'll be when I'm exhausted the next morning. I may have all of first period's papers graded, but if I can't teach with enthusiasm, then I've missed the purpose of teaching."

What is the purpose of being a Christian? Is it to get "everything" done? Or is it to live with purpose, with peace, and with confidence, so you can spend your time being a productive child of God? Learn and practice this vital spiritual discipline of being still before God so that you can hear his gentle, loving voice and know his will for your life.

Be still now for a moment and focus on
God telling you to,

"Relax my child, I have everything under my control. Remember, I Am God! Rest for a moment now in my loving arms."

IV

The Practical Process of Achieving Stillness with God

9

HOW TO BE STILL PHYSICALLY

God has made us a whole person consisting of spirit, soul (equals mind), and body (1 Thess. 5:23). They are not separate but one. Whenever we try to separate and isolate one or the other, we take away from the oneness and wholeness of a person. However, at times we have to address the separate aspects of our human life. I will describe the three components as they relate to God's design and the need to make time to be still and get some rest, as Jesus prescribes.

Remember the greatest commandment: Love the Lord your God with all your heart and with all your soul and with all your mind (Matt. 22:37; Deut. 6:4). We are a complete entity created by God and must incorporate our whole being in this process of meditating on God and being still in his presence. When one part of our being is affected, the rest of our being is affected physically, emotionally, and spiritually.

Awareness

The first step to improve our life with God is *awareness*. How are we doing physically?

We live in a stressed-filled society that has many negative

effects on us physically, emotionally, and spiritually. When we do not take time out and rest, we are affected by accumulated daily stress. Everyone experiences stress on a continual basis—stress with work, school, traffic, relationships, projects, crises, family, kids, or finances. You can have stress (eustress) from positive events like a marriage, a promotion, and a new house, or you can have stress (distress) from negative events in your life like the death of a loved one, the breakup of a relationship, injury, illness, financial loss, or problems with family members. Stress cannot be avoided. We must deal effectively with stress, or it can affect us in many negative ways. Stress can affect our physical and spiritual well-being, our thinking, and our relationships.

Let's look at some Biblical examples of people under stress. Notice how physically, emotionally, and spiritually, stress affects them, and how if physical stress is increased, so is emotional and spiritual stress.

Elijah

Elijah was told by an angel of God to get up and eat when Elijah was feeling weak and discouraged (1 Kings 19:5-8). He did not feel like continuing on and wanted to give up. After he felt better physically and was strengthened, he continued his journey and mission for God.

We see how Elijah (See 1 Kings 18-19) was under a great deal of stress. He experienced good stress when he was victorious over the prophets of Baal and negative stress when people wanted to kill him. Elijah became *physically* too weak to travel to the mountain of God. Elijah also became *emotionally* affected to the point of severe depression and had thoughts wanting to die (Elijah "prayed that he might die." "Take my life." 1 Kings 19: 4). This affected him *spiritually* to where he felt he was the only godly person left. He felt he was alone without anyone to support him (1 Kings 19:10).

How do you feel spiritually when you are not feeling well

physically? There could be many reasons for not feeling physically well, but the most common reason is stress exhaustion. Becoming exhausted due to stress can cause many physical problems besides affecting you emotionally and spiritually.

Many times after "mountaintop experiences," we are drained and experience self-doubt, physical weakness, and discouragement. Some modern-day mountaintop experiences include a child's wedding, winning a race, having a baby, and getting a promotion at work. Often, there are added responsibilities.

Jesus

We even see Jesus experiencing great distress before he was arrested and crucified (Matt. 26:38). At first he prayed that God would take away the suffering he was about to experience, even though he wanted to do the will of the Father. Jesus' spirit was filled with such agony and anguish. He said his soul was deeply sorrowful, and he was filled with strong, loud crying and tears (Heb. 5:7). Jesus was so stressed out that his sweat was like drops of blood falling to the ground (Luke 22:44).

This is an actual physical phenomenon. Either his sweat became so profuse that every drop was as large as a drop of blood, or, as the physician Luke writes about the account, Jesus' sweat was mixed with actual blood. People under great mental stress can break out in a bloody sweat from their pores becoming so dilated that blood may come through them, mixing with the sweat.

God sent an angel to strengthen Jesus in his time of despair. He did not give in to the stress and weakness of the moment, even though he fully experienced what must be close to the limit of human physical stress, but rather he trusted in God, his Father (Luke 22:42ff).

However, Jesus' disciples could not stay physically, emotionally or spiritually awake. In the garden with Jesus, they fell asleep from their stress and sorrow (Luke 22:45). Eventually they all deserted Jesus and ran (Matt. 26:56). This is what we tend to do when we are under stress and do not turn to God. We grow weak in our faith and run away.

The Effects Of Stress

We need to be aware of how stress is affecting us and then do something about it. Take this physical inventory to see how you might be affected by stress.

Stress-Exhaustion Symptoms
(Physical)

____stroke	____ulcers
____fatigue	____fidgety
____asthma	____arthritis
____insomnia	____back pains
____bronchitis	____indigestion
____chest pain	____restlessness
____headaches	____heart disease
____clumsiness	____teeth grinding
____low energy	____upset stomach
____weight change	____accident prone
____pounding heart	____slower reflexes
____appetite change	____dropping things
____muscle soreness	____premature aging
____muscle weakness	____foot/finger tapping
____muscle tension and tightness	____high blood pressure
____proneness to colds and allergies	
____increased alcohol, drug, tobacco use	

Any of these symptoms can be caused or made worse by stress. We need to find healthy, effective ways to relieve stress. Was Jesus concerned with relieving stress and with getting some rest? Absolutely! (See Chapter eight.)

The Ultradian Principle

There is a physical science that explains how God has designed us. Understanding this biological science, how the human body was created, and how it operates, can help us deal with stress better.[1]

Generally, our body and mind operate for about 90 to 120 minutes before starting to enter a period of low energy, called a trough. It is during this trough that we feel tired and worn out, and we tend to daydream or fantasize. During this time, it is difficult to concentrate and remember things. We may feel "spaced out," make more errors, and be clumsier than normal. We may feel more irritable, angry, or sleepy. It can also be a time when we give in to temptation and sin more easily.

Scientifically, these cycles or rhythms are called *ultradian rhythms*, because they occur more than once a day. (You are probably more familiar with circadian rhythms, which occur once a day like our sleep and wakefulness cycle.) Our ultradian cycles affect our organs, glands, muscles, blood, hormones, and our immune system that reaches down to our cells and genes. Therefore, our whole being (body, mind, and spirit) is affected by these rhythms throughout the day. These ultradian rhythms oscillate like a bell curve, reaching a peak in energy before sliding down into a low-energy trough. Our energy cycle may vary between 90 and 120 minutes because it depends on the type of activity we are doing. Obviously the more demanding the activity, the shorter our energy will last before it needs to be replenished.

Unfortunately, most of us do not take any time out to recharge, especially not to spend quiet, intimate time with God in prayer and meditation. The world's demands and pressures seduce us. We therefore tend to ignore our God-created internal signals to take a break, come to him, and be renewed for his glory and praise.

A major researcher of these ultradian rhythms, Ernest Rossi, writes, "We try to avoid our normal 20-minute break that nature is calling for, because we regard it as an inconvenience or a weakness."[2] God has built into us these biological rhythms. Did God design us this way to remind us to stop from our busyness of the day and turn to him for our renewal? We know how he told us in the Pentateuch that he made the seventh day for rest. We also know how the apostle Paul tells us to pray without ceasing (1 Thess. 5:17). We experience a trough in our energy six to eight times a day. Wouldn't these be good times to go to God in prayer and allow him to recharge us as we rest in him?

While I was teaching a Bible class on this material, a woman in class who teaches special education told me of how she applied these principles of slowing down, taking time out, and relying on God for peace. Once there was a disturbed child in her class who would not stop screaming. This woman became very upset and unsettled. She remembered how she could turn to Jesus and be still. She repeated, "Be still, be still," as she became aware of God's presence, power, and peace. Soon, she felt a great peace from God, and she was then able to deal with the child in a calm, confident way.

Biologically, the rest period of the ultradian trough lasts about 20 minutes. This is the ideal time needed to be recharged and rejuvenated. It takes the body and the mind about 20 minutes to replenish the used-up energy from our cells from the previous 90 to 120 minutes of activity.

It is also about every 90 to 120 minutes, that we get hungry and have to use the restroom. The healthiest way to live is in compliance with how God designed us. However, we tend to violate many of these principles. We should take a break every 90 to 120 minutes. We should eat every 90 to

120 minutes in small, healthy portions. Most health experts recommend eating five to six small meals throughout the day. This alone will make us healthier and less affected by stress. These biological principles can be utilized just on a physical basis for improved health. However, we can make further use of these natural principles if we meditate on God and be fully restored, not only naturally, but also supernaturally (spiritually) by God.

For most people, there is a certain time of the day that is usually the most difficult to get through. You feel like you are really dragging and worn out. This time averages between three and four o'clock in the afternoon. Two Japanese ultradian researchers, Yoichi Tsuji and Toshinori Kobayshi, have called this time "the *breaking point*."[3]

Some countries honor these natural rhythms intuitively. For example, England usually has a tea time between 3 P.M. and 4 P.M. Countries like Mexico and Spain have a siesta time in the middle of the afternoon. They may not know about the science behind these natural rhythms, but they are in tune with how their body and mind function.

The practical application of these God-designed ultradian rhythms is to first become aware of them in your own life, then make use of them.

Signs Of An Ultradian Trough

Here are some of the signs that you are entering an ultradian trough and need to take a physical, emotional, and spiritual break.

1. Feeling a need to relax
2. Staring into space
3. More difficulty concentrating
4. Yawning
5. Feeling a need to stretch
6. Needing to use the restroom

7. Slower reflexes, even clumsiness
8. A growling stomach, hunger pangs
9. Absent-minded doodling
10. Sleepiness or daydreaming
11. Making more mistakes
12. Feeling a need to stop work
13. Feeling a need to guzzle coffee or cola
14. Feeling a need to eat snacks
15. Feeling more impatient

Become aware of your own signs or cues telling you that you need a break. Let this time serve as a reminder of how God wants you to come to him to find rest for your weary soul. This is a time when it is *easier* to be still and just meditate on God's word, works, or wonders. Use this time to feel God's presence and be renewed by him.

Come to me all who are weary and burdened and I will give you rest. (Matt. 11:28)

Come with me by yourselves to a quiet place and get some rest. (Mark 6:31)

Be still and know that I am God. (Ps. 46:10)

Practical Applications

Slowing down and taking a break is difficult for many people, especially in our fast-paced society. We can and must change our lifestyle into a less stressful one by using these ultradian breaks. We tend to associate relaxation with sleep or goofing off. We may also have uncomfortable issues to deal with as we relax. But, if God himself needed to rest from his work, how much more do we? We must learn how to relax in life, in our wakeful times.

Here are some practical *physical* tips on how to slow down, be still, and know God. Some of these tips can be combined. The main thing is to find which method(s) help you to slow down to focus on God and feel his ever-loving presence. These ultradian tips that follow can be used in conjunction with the basic meditative tips found in *chapter four*. The tips in this present chapter and the next two chapters are applications that use our natural ultradian rhythms that God created within us. Taking these ultradian breaks is very beneficial whether a person uses them in a spiritual way or in a non-spiritual way. Some of the following tips are healthy in general without necessarily focusing on God such as in No. 4, 8-11.

1. Take a brief *"ultradian nap"* as you focus your attention on the love of God. This should last approximately twenty minutes.

2. Take your deepest twenty-minute ultradian break of the day (perhaps even a nap if you need one) during the *"breaking point."* Remember, this is usually around 3 P.M. to 4 P.M. This is usually the most difficult time of the day to get through.

3. *Schedule* an ultradian break at the end of the workday before you go home if possible. This will make you a much better person when you arrive home after a stressful day at work.

4. *Take* a twenty-minute nap when you first get home from work if you couldn't take one at work. Plan it out with your family. You and your family will notice the difference.

5. *Use* a portion of your lunch hour for an ultradian spiritual break. *Get away* from the workplace if possible and practice some of the ideas mentioned, according to what is feasible for you to do. *Focus* on nondemanding tasks during your ultradian restoration periods.

6. Keep paper and pen at hand to *jot down* ideas, in-

sights, and convictions when coming out of a twenty-minute break. This method will help you retain those special insights you received during this time.

7. *Organize* your work plan for the next day while you are in a trough.

8. *Engage* in light reading and other nurturing activities that gently support you, but do not tax your strength.

9. *Engage* in nonstressful conversation or quiet activity.

10. *Maximize* the benefits of your trough. Do nurturing and restorative activities such as working on a favorite hobby, listening to music, reading, light socializing, and meditating.

11. Have a *light, healthy snack* containing no more than 200 to 300 calories. Sugary snacks are not a good idea because they only give you a short energy high. Afterward, you feel as if you need more sugar to achieve that same high.

When You Can't Take a 20- Minute Break

Take a mini-ultradian break (a three-or five-minute break may be enough at times): phase out—just stare out into space and give yourself a rest. You can apply some of the ideas mentioned previously that would fit into your situation.

Take an Active Ultradian Break. Change your pace or take a break from concentrated, more demanding types of work. Some of the items mentioned previously would be considered active (No. 7 through No. 11).

Examples Of An Active Ultradian Break

1. Puttering or doodling
2. Talking casually to a co-worker
3. Making personal telephone calls
4. Taking a short walk through the office or shop
5. Stretching and taking a few deep breathes
6. Doing some routine filing or reorganization tasks
7. Going to the bathroom
8. Getting something to eat
9. Saying a prayer

Certain Activities Are Counterproductive During Active Ultradian Breaks

1. Strenuous exercise
2. Rushed activities
3. Highly directed kind of work
4. Machinery operation
5. Time-pressure tasks
6. Decision making
7. New creative work

If you are an ultradian break beginner, you can start with a short break every 90 to 120 minutes. Gradually, you can increase your quiet time with God from five minutes, to ten minutes, and eventually to twenty minutes. Soon you will build a closer, intimate relationship with God. Use these continual energy troughs to cue you to rest in him and gain your strength and confidence from him.

So, the next time you start to feel as if you need a break, stop what you are doing, and spend the time in solitude, being still and quiet while you meditate on the Lord. Just sit still in his presence and let him speak to your heart as he transforms you into his likeness (2 Cor. 3:18).

23rd Psalm for Busy People

The Lord is my pacesetter, I shall not rush.
He makes me stop and rest for quiet intervals,
He provides me with images of stillness
Which restore my serenity.
He leads me in ways of efficiency,
through calmness of mind,
And His guidance is peace.
Even though I have a great many
things to accomplish this day
I will not fret, His all-importance
will keep me in balance.
He prepares refreshment and renewal
in the midst of my activity
By anointing my mind with the oils of tranquility.

My cup of joyous energy overflows.
Surely harmony and effectiveness shall
be the fruits of my hours.
For I shall walk in the pace of my Lord,
And dwell in His house forever.

Source Unknown

10

How to Be Still Emotionally

To be still emotionally may be one of life's greatest difficulties. We may be able to slow our bodies down physically, but our emotions are still stirring within us. Have you ever lain in bed late at night, exhausted physically, but unable to stop your mind from thinking? How can we find mental peace?

We have seen in the previous chapter that our body and mind need a resting period to recharge the energy molecules that restore our strength and ability to deal with our activities more effectively. The longer we neglect taking a rest, the more damage is done by the build up of stress and the depletion of our energy reserves.

We saw some possible physical signs in chapter nine that told us when to take a break. In this chapter, we will look at some emotional, mental, and relational signs that tell us we need to take care of something. The same treatment is needed, which is to have quiet time with God. This allows God to work through us naturally, by our normal bodily restoration process, and supernaturally, by his Spirit who transforms us into God's likeness (2 Cor. 3:18).

Now take an emotional inventory of yourself.

Stress-Exhaustion Symptoms
(Emotional, Mental, Relational)

Emotional

____jealous ____jumpy
____fearful ____yelling
____irritable ____distrustful
____anxious ____discouraged
____envious ____self-doubting
____resentful ____feeling helpless
____impatient ____feeling hopeless
____frustrated ____feeling poor self-esteem
____worrying ____thinking impure thoughts
____easily-angered ____losing temper more easily
____crying more easily ____having obsessive thinking
____having unwanted thoughts
____feeling down and depressed

Mental

____bored ____distracted
____lethargic ____uncreative
____forgetful ____spacing out
____confused ____easily distracted
____unfocused ____having mental blocks
____unproductive ____making more mistakes
____mentally-tired ____frequently daydreaming
____negative in attitude ____misplacing/losing things
____having a racing mind ____making careless mistakes
____having difficulty concentrating
____having difficulty making decisions
____having difficulty organizing things

Relational

____rude	____unkind
____harsh	____jealous
____hiding	____envious
____lonely	____isolated
____resentful	____nagging
____intolerant	____impatient
____untrusting	____indifferent
____suspicious	____unforgiving
____lashing out	____self-seeking
____"clamming up"	____not intimate
____easily-angered	____using people
____holding grudges	____more-withdrawn
____more argumentative	
____more easily annoyed by others	

How many of these symptoms do you experience? How many messages is God sending you through the design of your body, emotions, and spirit? The more we ignore these signs and symptoms, the more prone we are to suffer from them.

Obstacles to Being Still Emotionally

There are many obstacles that prevent people from being still emotionally. When we try to become still, quiet, and silent, many of our buried and unresolved emotional issues surface. This can be a very disturbing and uncomfortable experience. It is tempting to keep busy rather than deal with our uncomfortable feelings.

There are many ways we can seek relief from our emotional issues. A few examples of temporary relief include involvement in activities, busyness, chaos, drugs, alcohol, sex, achievements, education, projects, work, medications, and food. Most of these attempted solutions are temporary, super-ficial, and destructive. Later, these solutions can become ad-dictions.

The addictive process provides an escape from our pain instead of dealing with it. Most people in the western world have addictions of some kind. Our souls are restless, and many do not know how to still the troubled, emotional wa-ters. Until we can become still and know God personally, we will remain restless, unfulfilled, and dissatisfied. We have to have a replacement for our addiction that truly fulfills and satisfies.

God's Solution

God knows what will work for us. He wants us to have an abundant life in him. When we are able to spend even 20 minutes meditating on God, when we trust him to the point of really being open, we may find ourselves blissfully falling in love! The cares of the world fade away as we feel secure in the loving arms of God. We begin to gain a deeper appre-ciation of his sovereignty, realizing that he is in control and will take care of us.

Many people are realizing the need for a spiritual life and are seeking transformation. They are turning to various phi-losophies and New Age methods and techniques. These ap-proaches may give a sense of peace and healing, but it is false and short-lived, because the loneliness of our hearts is still not addressed. Only that which is eternal and from God will fulfill our deepest need of love and life. We continue searching all areas of life like Solomon did, finally realizing that all is useless and meaningless without knowing God. God has designed us with a core need for him and things that are eternal. God has set eternity in the hearts of people (Ec-cles. 3:11). Therefore, only the divine eternal healing that comes from the one true God, who demonstrated his reality to us through the resurrection of his Son Jesus Christ, can give true transformation and satisfaction. We have been conditioned and convinced that our transformation and healing is within our own power. That's what secular humanism teaches. That's what modern psychology teaches. They teach that we are our own god.

Realizing that the power of transformation comes from God (and God alone) through Jesus Christ, we must come to him in full surrender and trust. However, this is not easy. First, it is not easy to be still. Second, it is not easy to be very intimate with the Almighty God. It wasn't easy for the many people in the Bible as was mentioned earlier in this book. The Israelites were not prepared to face God one on one. They told Moses to "speak to us yourself and we will listen. But do not have God speak to us or we will die" (Exod. 20:19).

God's instructions really do demand that we die—die to ourselves. That is the price and the blessing of wonderful, God-given, long-sought-for peace. We are told to "not conform any longer to the pattern of this world, but be transformed by the renewing of your mind" (Rom. 12:2a). It is at this time that we are then able to see clearer in a spiritual way and realize and appreciate how God's will is good, pleasing, and perfect (Rom. 12:2b).

We become like the bright moon in its full phase. The moonlight does not originate from the moon, but rather from the sun. The moon has no light of itself. The bright moonlight at night is just a reflection from the sun. All the moon has to do is come into the presence of the sun so it can reflect the sun's light.

Likewise, all we have to do is come into the presence of God, and he does the transforming (2 Cor. 3:18). So what do we do with our fears and emotional traumas that begin to surface, our restlessness, our anxiety, our depression, or any other uncomfortable, painful, or frightening emotion that arise as we become still and silent before God?

First we *realize* and become *aware* that we may experience discomfort—physically, emotionally, or spiritually. The sin, past trauma, unresolved issues, anger, hurt, and so forth, begin to arise and are manifested in many different ways. When you begin to notice any signs or symptoms physically, emotionally, or spiritually, *use* those symptoms as messengers to tell you that some things need to be taken care of. *Greet* the discomfort and use it. Realize that the discomfort is a sign that the deep issues are beginning to be addressed and resolved. You may feel like crying. You may begin to feel frightened. You may not want to be completely overwhelmed. You can take it slow. Realize that God is working with you and through you to *heal* and *transform* you. As you slowly face your discomfort and fears, you face God and draw near to him. He is transforming you. Transformation for anything is a struggle, but this is a different type of struggle. It is a struggle that will produce resolution, as you confront your fears and are freed from the bondage that Satan has wrapped you in all these years. As you begin to trust God and rely on him for your safety, security, acceptance, forgiveness, and love, the more you will be able to let go and allow God to transform you into his likeness—a likeness not ruled by addiction, fear, or stress.

The Bible tells how Jesus struggled and agonized in prayer. His sweat became like drops of blood as he was in anguish praying to God the Father. He understands our struggles. You can go slowly with the process. The Bible indicates that this transformation is a continual process. We are being transformed into his likeness on a daily basis (2 Cor. 3:18). The more you become intimate and still before God, the more you trust and love him for who he is, and the more you submit to his Spirit. The more you develop your intimate love with God, the more your fear goes away. Remember that perfect love casts out all fear (I John 4:18).

So let go and allow God to take over. Surrender to him so he can transform and heal you. Give yourself time to continue through the various experiences. Write down what you experience after twenty minutes in stillness with God. Remember God is working on you and through you. You have to allow the Divine Healer to operate on your body, mind, and spirit, and be ready for joy to come! Remember the verse, "Sorrow may endure for a night, but joy comes in the morning" (Ps. 30:5).

Practical Applications

Here are some practical tips to help you slow down mentally and emotionally. Some of these tips can be combined. The main thing is to find which method(s) help you to slow down to focus on God and feel his ever-loving presence. These ultradian tips that follow can be used in conjunction with the basic meditative tips found in *chapter four*.

These tips will help you to share your grief with God and to be open to healing, precisely because you are opening yourselves to full communion with the one who loves you the most.

1. Focus on things in slow motion or things that help slow down your mind and emotions. When your mind is going fast, it is difficult to relax.
2. Meditate on a comforting portion of Scripture. It may be a word, phrase, or a larger section. I have memorized Psalm 23 and enjoy repeating that Psalm continually until I drift off in peacefulness with God for about twenty minutes. Repeat a comforting word or phrase that is soothing to you.
3. You may read through the Psalms until you come upon one that expresses how you are feeling, whether they are pleasant or unpleasant feelings. This can be used as a way to express whatever you are feeling to God so that he can ultimately comfort you.
4. Concentrate on a very relaxing scene where you enjoy God's serenity, support, security, and safety. The scene may be on a warm, sunny beach or in the

cool, refreshing mountains. Allow the scene to unfold and become vivid. Put yourself in the scene and look through your eyes to see all the beauty of the scene.

- See all the colors.
- Hear all the comforting serene sounds.
- Smell the fresh air.
- Feel the soothing experience.
- Taste the clean air.

Use all five senses to vividly experience the scene with yourself there. Make it come to life. Praise God for the experience.

5. Know that your counselor, your perfect father, your Song-of-Solomon lover, your friend, is also your Creator. To know him as GOD. To know that really and truly this magnificent being who could be the meanest totalitarian the universe has ever known is instead love and peace. Love and peace he wants you to choose. We have a right to that choice. Isn't that amazing?

Remember, you may start out with five minutes a day practicing being still and quiet before God. With time, practice and healing, you will be able to sit in quietness with God for longer periods of time. Work your way up to at least two twenty-minute breaks a day with God. Ultimately and according to our ultradian design, we can use a twenty-minute break with God every 90 to 120 minutes throughout the day.

Take time to be holy.

11

How to Be Still Spiritually

To be still spiritually may be the most difficult. The deeper we get to our core being which is our soul, the more discomfort we may experience. The reason for this is because the soul reveals the deepest truths about our relationship with God. All is exposed at the spiritual level. We cannot hide or avoid anything. We have no self-defenses to protect us against our dark, unwanted side. All is laid bare before God. Our true self is exposed, and our false self can no longer serve us.

Trying to be still spiritually before God means we will be humbled and stripped of our defenses that attempt to hide our false self. Adam and Eve tried to hide from God because of their sin. They covered themselves trying to hide their shame and vulnerabilities. We must regain our trust in God so we can come to God openly and honestly. The more we spend time with God intimately, the more we will grow to know him personally and trust him. We will feel more safe and secure with him. We will experience his love and grace in a deeper way.

Our Cover-Up

Let's first become aware of how we tend to cover ourselves, which interferes with our level of intimacy with God, others, and ourselves.

On the physical level we can modify, cover up or hide physical features we do not like. We can put on a smile even when we are hurting and crying on the inside. We can disguise or try to transfigure ourselves by our own means to try to feel better. We can try new diets, new exercise equipment, new workout plans, cosmetic surgeries, and new clothes. However, the change is only surface deep, and maybe skin deep. These changes do not heal the deep, inner longing of our soul, which only God and his eternal power can fulfill through an intimate relationship with him.

Emotionally we can try to feel better and be transformed. We can read all the latest self-help books, go to the best psychotherapists, and boost our self-esteem. We can build up psychological defenses to hide our inner weaknesses and hurts. We can appear emotionally strong and brave on the surface while trying to fool others and ourselves of our vulnerabilities, but we still are not at peace with ourselves, others, or with God.

Intellectually, we can go to the best schools and get all A's and receive great honors. However, even these people commit suicide at times. King Solomon searched all areas of life to the extreme of our wildest fantasies and concluded that all is useless, meaningless, and empty without taking care of the core essential of life (Eccles. 1:2). All that matters is having the right relationship with God (Eccles. 12:13).

Our environment, society, family, and heredity going back to Adam and Eve infect us. We are infected with a compulsive nature to try to modify our false self. This is the self that is not real and separated from God. The false self builds defenses so people cannot see the true self. We are afraid of people seeing our real or true self for fear we will not be accepted.

The greatest discomfort and most tragic experience is to find yourself empty and cut off from our source of life—God—to the point where our soul cries out, "My God, my God, why have you abandoned me?" Even while we attempt to be still and quiet before God we occasionally feel separated and lonely.

At the climax of God's grace and love for the world, Jesus found himself in darkness and despair (Matt. 27:45-46), crying out in a loud voice, "Eloi, Eloi, lama sabachthani?" which translates, "My God, my God, why have you forsaken me?" The whole land actually experienced darkness for three hours during this time. It was one of the darkest days on earth for the world and for Jesus. However, since we know the rest of the story, we know that transition, transfiguration, and transformation soon took place.

Our Transformation

The resurrection of Jesus Christ, the Son of God Almighty, was the greatest event in all history. Through Jesus, God shows how we go through desert experiences (See Matt. 4:1-11), sufferings (See Heb. 5:7-8), great anguish (See Luke 22:44), and darkness and despair (See Matt. 22:45-46). All these experiences can lead us to full dependency and trust in God. Jesus is our example. He learned obedience from what he suffered even to the point of death (Phil. 2:8).

One of the challenges of being still before God is suffering through these uncomfortable experiences. St. John of the Cross (a sixteenth century Carmelite monk)[1] describes the experience of solitude and stillness with God where one may feel a sense of dryness or loneliness, which he calls the "Dark Night of the Spirit." St. John of the Cross describes this experience as a time of purification where the false self is eliminated. He says:

Oh, then, spiritual soul, when you see your appetites darkened, your inclinations dry and constrained, your faculties incapacitated for any interior exercise, do not be afflicted; think of this as a grace, since God is freeing you from yourself and taking from you your own activity.[2]

When we stand in the presence of God in stillness and quietness, we are stripped of our pride and humbled by his awesomeness.

We have become attached, dependent, and addicted to our false self and all its defenses, justifications, rationalizations, and excuses. Thus, when we begin to dismantle our false self, we feel vulnerable, afraid, insecure, alone, and even lost. It is very difficult to be still during this time. However, we must recognize these signs as healing messages if we are relying on God to transform us by his power and Spirit (2 Cor. 3:18). We must realize that "the dark night of the spirit" is one of the ways God works with us in our transformation. We must not give up on our spiritual journey when we experience these symptoms. When we prolong these phases of dryness, powerlessness, and (even as with Jesus on the cross) a sense of being abandoned by God, we realize that God is working on us and purging us of our false self. Because we are so attached to our false self, we tend to almost grieve its loss—or as with an addiction, we go through withdrawal-type symptoms when we shed our false self. We must always stay focused on God as our Divine Healer and friend who knows what is best, because he will see us through these "dark nights" of our spiritual journey, just as he did with Jesus Christ.

Just as we found in the chapters on physical and emotional effects of stress and busyness, first we need to become aware of how we are affected spiritually by the common stresses of life.

Now take a spiritual inventory of yourself.

Stress-Exhaustion Symptoms
(Spiritual)

___doubtful
___apathetic
___undirected
___feeling dry
___purposeless
___unforgiving
___lacking faith
___feeling alone
___feeling empty
___empty
___not desiring to go to church
___not desiring to read the Bible
___not desiring to go to Bible class
___feeling as if you are in a dark cloud
___looking for magical or exciting answers
___not desiring to be around other spiritual people

___joyless
___cynical
___rebellious
___feeling lost
___disobedient
___feeling useless
___meaninglessness
___lacking ambition
___not desiring to pray
___feeling no one cares
___wanting a quick thrill

You can experience any of these symptoms when you neglect being still and quiet before God. The further we drift away from God, the more we tend to sin. On the other hand, you can experience some of these symptoms as you draw near to God. The only difference is that one direction leads to healing and transformation, and the other direction leads to sickness, debilitation, and death.

Our spiritual transformation will bring us to closer intimacy with God, leading to a greater love for him. His love never changes for us. He always loves us unconditionally. As we develop our love for God by spending quiet, intimate time with him, we become less fearful of our insecurities. Perfect love drives out fear (1 John 4:18).

So how do we slow down and become still and quiet with God in solitude, prayer, and biblical meditation?

We first realize our need to slow down from the symptoms of stress we experience physically, emotionally and spiritually. We then realize our need for God to provide for us as we practice being still and quiet with him.

Practical Applications

1. We can begin to be still by reading various Scriptures, especially ones that remind us about being still and relying on God for rest, renewal, restoration, and strength.

   Come to me, all you who are weary and burdened, and I will give you rest. Take my yoke upon you and learn from me, for I am gentle and humble in heart, and you will find rest for your souls. For my yoke is easy and my burden is light. (Matt.11:28-30)

   Be still and know that I am God. (Ps. 46:10)

   Be still before the Lord and wait patiently for Him. (Ps. 37:3)

2. Meditate on God's Word

   Oh how I love your law! I meditate on it all day long. (Ps. 119:97)

   Let the word of Christ dwell in you richly... (Col. 3:16)

As you meditate on God's Word and allow it to seep deeply within your soul, you can gradually become more still in his holy presence. This may take some time with practice and discipline to stop our own efforts and just be still before God.

   He gives strength to the weary and increases the

power of the weak. Even youths grow tired and weary, and young men stumble and fall; but those who hope in the Lord will renew their strength. They will soar on wings like eagles; they will run and not grow weary, they will walk and not faint. (Isa. 40:29-31)

So do not fear, for I am with you; do not be dismayed, for I am your God. I will strengthen you and help you; I will uphold you with my righteous right hand. (Isa. 41:10)

I will refresh the weary and satisfy the weak. (Jer. 31:25)

God wants us to take a break from our busyness and come to him for renewal, recharging, and transformation. It is God who leads us if we will follow.

He makes me lie down in green pastures, he leads me beside quiet waters, he restores my soul. He guides me in paths of righteousness for his name's sake. (Ps. 23:2-3)

THE CHRISTIAN SPIRITUAL JOURNAL

Another important spiritual exercise is what I call the *Christian Spiritual Journal*, based on the ultradian principle and God's Word. This is a self-contained spiritual exercise that summarizes the main message in this book in becoming intimate with God. You may copy this section and put it on your refrigerator or in your Bible to practice daily. This spiritual exercise first reminds you of some relevant Scriptures concerning the commands, examples, and the need to be still and to know God personally. Meditate on the Scriptures, with their blessings and commandments. You then can follow the four-step outline below to be more open to God's mighty transforming power.

Biblical Commands

Be still and know that I am God. (Ps. 46:10)

Be still before the Lord and wait patiently for him. (Ps. 37:7)

Be still before the Lord, all mankind. (Zech. 2:13)

Examples of Jesus finding rest and drawing close to the Father

And in the morning, a great while before day, he rose and went to a lonely place, and there he prayed. (Mark 1:35)

But he withdrew to the wilderness and prayed. (Luke 5:16)

In these days he went out to the mountain to pray: and all night he continued in prayer to God. (Luke 6:12)

And after he had taken leave of them, he went up on the mountain to pray. (Mark 6:46)

And after he had dismissed the crowds, he went up on the mountain himself to pray. When evening came, he was there alone. (Matt. 14:23)

Now it happened that as he was praying alone the disciples were with him; and he asked them, "Who do the people say that I am?" (Luke 9:18)

Now about eight days after saying this, he took with him Peter and John and James, and went up on the mountain to pray. (Luke 9:28)

And he said to them, "Come with me by yourselves to a quiet place and get some rest." (Mark 6:31)

Four-Step Outline for Spiritual Transformation

1. Become aware of your regular troughs throughout the day by noticing the indicative signs as described in chapter nine.
2. Allow yourself to experience the regular troughs by allowing your mind and body to go inward or transcend beyond the present time, or to experience the present moment fully—in other words, to become still before God and feel his presence. This may last approximately five to twenty minutes.
3. When you start to come out of your trough, take note of your experiences, thoughts and feelings. Notice any possible spiritual convictions, concerns, or insights.
4. Write down these experiences over several days or weeks and notice the various spiritual insights and developments you achieve.

This experience can help you develop a greater closeness to God.

Other Spiritual Disciplines

There are many ways you can begin to train and discipline yourself to be still and silent before God so that he can transform you into his likeness. Remember that this is a spiritual discipline that takes practice in how to listen and meditate with God rather than to rely on your own efforts. Look forward to being intimately united with God the Father through Jesus Christ and his Holy Spirit. Allow him to be active in your heart, soul, body, and mind for a supernatural transformation that can only come from God and not by anything we can do to make ourselves better. It is a gift of God. We just have to prepare ourselves to be open to his transforming power.

There are other spiritual disciplines that can help us in our relationship with God. These disciplines are ways to quiet the noise in our mind, body, and soul. We have been infected by noise that is actually embedded in our mind, body, and soul. The spiritual disciplines of prayer, fasting, and Bible study help us to purge the noise and pollution from the world out of our body, soul, and mind. We will look at these in the last three chapters.

V

From the Rooftop to the Mountaintop

12

Transformation Results

ow would you feel, as you are reading this chapter, if your phone rings and the voice on the other end addresses you by name and says, "This is the President of the United States. My wife and I would like to invite you to the White House for dinner to discuss your concerns about the way this country is being run. I will have a private plane pick you up tomorrow at 4:00 P.M."? Whether or not you like the president, how would you feel? Some feelings might be excitement, confusion, awe, or fear. You may ask yourself, "Why me?" Then when you actually meet the president face to face, and he shakes your hand and says, "I am glad that you can join us for dinner tonight," what kind of feelings or reactions would you experience? Maybe you would become speechless and not know what to say.

How would you feel if God appeared in your room tonight, called you by name, and said he would like to talk to you? Would you scream and run out of the house? Would you faint? Would you shake in your boots and stutter? Would you cry with joy or with fear? How excited would you be? Who can imagine how Samuel really felt? I can tell you one thing, you would never be the same after such an encounter.

We can describe various encounters people had up close and personal with God throughout the Scriptures and throughout history. However, unless you attempt to seek God earnestly and allow him to reveal himself to you personally, you may never know what on earth it is like to be in the presence of the Almighty God, Creator of the Universe.

As you practice the spiritual discipline of being still before God and prayerfully meditate on him in solitude, you can expect to experience a greater *awareness* of your condition in the eyes of God. The awareness can lead to a *conviction* of how you need God's grace to make you right before him. If you allow God to convict your heart, and you turn to him away from your own ways to his ways, then God will *heal* you, and you will be *transformed*. You will then be more equipped and ready for *God's mission* with your life.

> If my people, who are called by my name, will humble themselves and pray and seek my face and turn from their wicked ways, then I will hear from heaven and will forgive their sin and will heal their land. (2 Chron.7:14)

We have to face our need for forgiveness of sin before we can be intimate and humble, ready to truly listen to God.

Notice what happens in each case of a person coming into the presence of God. First, it is usually a *terrifying and humbling experience*. Then this experience can lead into: *Awareness, Conviction, Healing* (or *Transformation*), and a *Mission* from God.

We must also note that the reactions we are about to see are a result of sin in our life. Before sin, Adam and Eve walked with God in the Garden of Eden without fear and without shame. Once they sinned, they tried to hide themselves from God and cover up because they were afraid (Gen. 3:10). Because we have all sinned and fallen short of God's glory (Rom. 3:23), we have something to worry about until we find and receive the true cure of our sin disease. The cure is God's grace through the saving power of Jesus his Son (Rom. 3:24-26).

Let's look in on some personal encounters with God and be ready to meet him face to face.

Adam and Eve

After Adam and Eve's sin of disobedience, they encountered God personally and were frightened (Gen. 3:10). Adam and Eve became aware of their condition, that they were naked (Gen. 3:10). When we come before God and realize who he is, we become *aware* of our nakedness. We realize that we are empty-handed, have nothing to offer God on our own, and are completely at his mercy. We cannot bluff, deceive, or fool God. It doesn't matter if we think we are pleasing God and are righteous because we think we follow the right doctrine or because we are a "good" person. That does not cure the penalty of sin and separation with God. Only God can restore us to himself according to his mercy and grace. God wants from us a personal relationship through his Son, Jesus Christ. Nothing else can reconcile us to that wonderful relationship with God our father.

We may feel complacent because we think we have the right answers and are morally good. We may feel confident and look down at other people. We may even feel like the Pharisee, who posed and prayed, "Oh, God, I thank you that I am not like other people—robbers, crooks, adulterers, or heaven forbid, like this taxman. I fast twice a week and tithe on all my income" (Luke 18:11-12, MSG). When you realize you are in the presence of God, you are humbled before him. You become more like the taxman who stood at a distance.

The taxman slumped in the shadows, his face in his hands, not daring to look up, and said: "God, give mercy.

Forgive me, a sinner" (Luke 18:13, MSG). This was the man who went away justified before God (Luke 18:14), because he came to God and humbled himself.

Israelites

Imagine you are in beautiful Hawaii enjoying the scenery. You are visiting the volcanoes. The sun is shining, the weather is a perfect 75 degrees Fahrenheit, and you are very relaxed. Suddenly dark clouds start rolling in with loud crackling thunder and bright flashes of lightening. You hear a loud noise that almost deafens your ears. It sounds like someone is blowing a trumpet in your ear. The volcano in front of you starts to smoke, rumble, and erupt. How would you feel? Would you tremble with fear?

This is somewhat of the experience the Israelites had in Exod. 20:18-19. "When the people saw the thunder and lightning and heard the trumpet and saw the mountain in smoke, they trembled with fear. They stayed at a distance and said to Moses, 'Speak to us yourself and we will listen. But do not have God speak to us or we will die.'" These people experienced God. They were in his presence. However, they responded in fear for their lives because they did not really know God personally. They could not approach God as a friend and a lover. They gave that job to Moses. They did not fully know the perfect love of God that does away with all fear (I John 4:18).

The Israelites trembled with fear when they came into the presence of God. This is one of the reactions we might have when we try to be still and silent in God's presence. We may become so fearful that we give up and leave it to the preacher to commune with God, but we must move past that fear and into the knowledge of being joyful, knowing the love and gentleness that God has for us. God addresses this through the apostle Paul to Christians.

Paul

Paul was made blind for three days. Maybe this was to make Paul realize that he has been blind all his life on how he thought he was pleasing God. The first step in Paul's transformation knocked him off his feet when he encountered the living God (Acts 9:4).

Terrified and Humbled

The experience was a terrifying and humbling experience for this "great" religious leader. Even the men traveling with Paul were speechless (Acts 9:7).

Aware and Convicted

Paul was then convicted and in humility responded to the Lord. He obeyed the orders (Acts 9:5, 8, 9, 17-22). He followed the men into town and met with Ananias.

Healed and Transformed

Paul obeyed the Lord and was healed of his physical and spiritual blindness (Acts 9:17-19). He then got up and was baptized, now transformed into a child of God ready to carry out his true mission from God.

The Mission

This man is my chosen instrument to carry my name before the Gentiles and their kings and before the people of Israel. I will show him how much he must suffer for my name. (Acts 9:15-16)

After Paul was terrified, humbled, made aware, and convicted, healed, saved, and transformed, he proceeded at once with his mission (Acts 9:20). "[Paul] began to preach in the synagogues that Jesus is the Son of God" (Acts 9:20). Even with persecution, Paul "grew more and more powerful and baffled the Jews living in Damascus by proving that Jesus is the Christ" (Acts 9:22). This was Paul's experience when he came into the presence of God and was transformed.

If we continue through the uncomfortable experiences we will develop a deeper love, respect, and trust for God. Jesus says, "Come with me by yourself to a quiet place and get some rest" (Mk. 6:31). We must have still, quiet, meditative time with Jesus. He will take care of us and heal us.

Elijah

What did Elijah experience when he came into the presence of the Lord? We read about Elijah's experience in 1 Kings 19:11-13. We discussed earlier how God revealed himself to Elijah in a gentle whisper. We see that when Elijah finally heard God, Elijah covered up his face. Elijah also experienced fear and uncertainty. It was a terrifying and humbling experience for the prophet. The wind was stronger than a hurricane and tore the mountains apart and shattered the rocks. There was an earthquake that must have felt like the end of the world—but there was more to come. There was a fire. Elijah must have felt time after time that his own life was about to end. Then there was silence, and a peace came over the land. Elijah was probably shaking in his sandals, wondering what was next. It must have been very humbling to see the power of God.

Do you think God had his attention? What do you think about that grand entrance of God? In the still silence, there was that gentle whisper. This also frightened Elijah: "When Elijah heard it, he pulled his cloak over his face and went out and stood at the mouth of the cave" (1 Kings 19:13). But Elijah did not run from God. Elijah cautiously peeked out of his cave to listen to God. Do you need to come out of your dark, stone cave? Do you need to take the challenge to meet God personally and to be transformed? Jesus is standing at the door of your heart right now and knocking. If you become still, you can hear his voice as he is calling you.

Elijah was made aware of God's holy presence and could hear him. This intimate encounter Elijah had with God on Mount Sinai led to his transformation and renewal. He was then given his mission from God, which Elijah fulfilled (I Kings. 19:15-21).

Isaiah

The great prophet Isaiah also experienced God intimately and had uncomfortable feelings. In Isaiah 6:1-8, we see Isaiah's personal encounter with God. Isaiah saw the Lord seated on a throne, high and exalted, filling the temple with his almighty presence. The heavenly beings were worshipping God saying, "Holy, holy, holy is the Lord Almighty, the whole earth is full of his glory" (v. 3).

The whole temple shook and was filled with smoke. Notice Isaiah's reaction. He was filled with grief, guilt, and despair. Isaiah said while in the presence of the Almighty, "Woe to me!" He cried, "I am ruined! For I am a man of unclean lips, and I live among a people of unclean lips, and my eyes have seen the King, the LORD Almighty" (Isa. 6:5).

The Living Bible translates this verse as, "My doom is sealed, for I am a foul-mouthed sinner, a member of a sinful, foul-mouthed race; and I have looked upon the king, the Lord of heaven's armies." How do you feel when you become aware of God's presence? Some people feel God's presence in a church building. They react by trying to be on their best behavior, sweet and kind to everyone. They make sure they try not to swear in the church building. They may wait until they get into the car before being their typical, unpleasant self with their spouse or kids. However, as we become more in tune with God and grow more intimate with him, we realize that he is present everywhere we go.

> Where can I go from your Spirit?
> Where can I flee from your presence?
> If I go up to heaven, you are there;
> If I make my bed in the depths, you are there.
> (Psalm 139)

When we realize we are in the presence of God, we must be humbled. The more we spend in quiet time with God, we realize his presence is everywhere and we see his works and wonders. We realize that we are nothing compared to God and that we are sinful. Again, this is an uncomfortable feeling at first, until we can trust in an all-powerful, loving God who is not out to harm us, but to care for us. Isaiah first became *aware* of his human condition of sin before being *convicted* of his sin, which led to a *healing and transformation*. In order for us to be healed of any problem, we must first become aware that we have a problem.

As discussed in chapter six, people do not deal with the deepest longing in their soul, which is eternity (Eccles. 3:11b). This is one of the reasons why many do not and will not slow down to be still and silent, because then the deep yearnings of the heart arise. The eternity that God has planted in the hearts of everyone begins to make people a little restless. Isaiah did not run away from his uncomfortable experience. One of God's angels flew to Isaiah and touched Isaiah's mouth with a live, hot, burning coal and said, "See, this has touched your lips; your guilt is taken away and your sin is forgiven" (Isa. 6:6-7). The almighty God healed Isaiah. God is the divine healer and the only one who can heal us of our worst disease—sin.

Isaiah now could hear God and be ready for God's calling. Isaiah said that he "heard the voice of the Lord saying, 'Whom shall I send as a messenger to my people? Who will go?'" (Isa. 6:8). When we take time to be in the presence of God by being silent and still, we are preparing ourselves for his service. We don't retreat from the responsibilities of the world. We do not retreat to live in the desert for the rest of our lives. Rather, we are recharged, renewed, and re-strengthened for action. We gain the strength from God if we wait upon him (Isa. 40:31). We will soar on wings like eagles; we will run and not grow weary; we will walk and not be faint, God says (Isa. 40:31), but we must always go to God to be recharged.

Isaiah's response to knowing God was, "Here am I. Send me!"(v. 8). Isaiah was now zealous and on fire for the Lord. He is now willing and ready. Do you want to feel that fire for the Lord again? Do you want to regain your zeal and desire for the Lord God? Come and be reacquainted with God. Make a decision today to spend quiet, intimate time with him so that you can know him and trust him. Then you can be renewed in your spirit and transformed into his likeness with ever-increasing glory, which comes from the Lord, who is the Spirit (2 Cor. 3:18).

Once we are forgiven, God is not finished with us. He has a mission for you and me. He had a mission for Isaiah, but Isaiah had to be touched by God first. Are you ready to be touched by God, to be made aware, convicted, healed (or transformed), then ready to receive your personal mission from God?

Peter

The apostle Peter was another person who encountered God intimately on several occasions. In Luke 5:1-10, we see the people coming to Jesus to hear him teach. Peter did not appear to be a good listener like Mary, the sister of Martha. Peter was also not yet aware of the divinity and power of Jesus.

Some of Peter's difficulty of being aware of God's presence and power is not much different from our difficulty at times. Peter had fished hard all night and was probably tired, worn out, and irritable. He must have felt unproductive in his hard work because he did not catch any fish (Luke 5:5). Peter could have also been worrying about not catching any fish. He was probably wondering about his business and not listening closely to Jesus and how he provides for all our needs. Peter's mind must have been filled with preoccupations.

Do you ever feel that way? Do you worry about your job situation, wondering if you are part of the next layoff? If your business slows down, do you begin to panic and worry? Do these job setbacks take your mind and heart off of Jesus because you are too worried about the lack of success in your job? It is difficult to be in tune with God and hear him when we are tired, distracted, and overwhelmed as Peter could have felt in Luke 5 and as Martha probably felt in Luke 10:40.

It was probably difficult for Peter to even think of such a thing as falling to his knees and praying to God. What would all his buddies think? Not rough and tough Peter. He was a loud-mouthed, rugged fisherman who took pride in his work.

Peter was the kind of guy to knock himself out fishing all night to try to catch fish before he would fall to his knees and make a fool out of himself. I'm sure Peter, like some of us, would never stop to ask for directions while traveling. Is pride getting in your way, to fall to your knees and be intimate with God? What will it take to bring us to our knees?

Sometimes we, like Peter, have to first become aware of God's presence and power. Jesus knew this, and he told worn-out, tired, frustrated, hyper Peter to do some more fishing. "What? Are you crazy? You gotta be kidding me!" Peter didn't say these exact words, but he could have been thinking them. "Master, we've worked hard all night and haven't caught anything" (Luke 5:5).

Just imagine when you have that major project to complete, and it's getting late. You continually get distracted. You spend many hours and late nights trying to get things done. The next day your computer hard drive crashes, and you lose all the work you spent weeks developing. Then your boss comes into your office and says he wants you to move your office across town to a new location. You are now ready to explode, but you listen because he is your boss and can fire you. You keep your cool and move to the new office building. When you get there, you notice it has all new equipment, a computer, large windows to look outside, a private bathroom, and outdoor patio. You turn on the computer and discover that all your work has been saved to that computer. You are amazed and ecstatic. Seem impossible? Not with Jesus as your boss.

Peter also reluctantly obeyed his Master, Jesus. "But because you say so, I will let down the nets" (Luke 5:5). Peter thought he would appease his Master. Peter didn't expect to catch anything, but Jesus had a lesson to teach Peter.

Suddenly their nets filled up with so many fish that the nets began to break (Luke 5:6). Immediately they called for help from James and John (Luke 5:7, 10) to use both boats to fill with the fish. It must have been chaos with the fish jumping all around and Peter very excited.! The boats were so full that they began to sink (Luke 5:7).

Aware and Convicted

It finally hit Peter. He was astonished (Luke 5:9). "When Simon Peter saw this, he fell at Jesus' knees" (Luke 5:8). Jesus had to show Peter a miracle by blessing his business tremendously with such a large catch of fish that their nets began to break and their boats began to sink. Now Peter becomes aware! Notice he goes from calling Jesus, "Master" (v. 5) to "Lord" (v. 8). Peter is aware that he is in the presence of the Holy One. Peter has seen the power of God at work in Jesus. Then, like Isaiah, Peter was convicted. Big, rough and tough Peter fell at Jesus' knees and said, "Go away from me, Lord, I am a sinful man!" (v. 8).

What God desires is for us to "act justly and to love mercy and to walk humbly with your God" (Micah 6:8). The sacrifices that God wants from us are a broken spirit, and a broken and contrite heart (Psalm 51:17). The Lord is compassionate and loving to the humble in heart. While Peter was on his knees realizing what a sinful man that he was, Jesus said to Peter, "Don't be afraid" (Luke 5:16).

What a comfort to have a personal Savior who wants to call us his friend and brother. We have a Savior and God who cares about us.

The Mission

Now that Peter is *aware, convicted,* and *healed,* he is ready for his *mission* from God. Jesus tells Peter, "from now on you will catch men" (Luke 5:10). Peter immediately follows. "So they pulled their boats up on shore, left everything and followed [Jesus]" (Luke 5:11).

When we spend personal and intimate time with God, we begin to realize what is important and everlasting. Our whole perspective is changed. Peter was ready to give up his whole business, once he realized he was in the presence of God. He was this open to God's calling to save people. He found true life and its meaning by coming to know the giver of eternal life. Come to God and hear what plans he has for you:

> For I know the plans I have for you, declares the LORD, plans to prosper you and not harm you, plans to give you hope and a future. Then you will call upon me and come and pray to me, and I will listen to you. You will seek me and find me when you seek me with all your heart. (Jeremiah 29:11)

At first we may feel terrified in our intimate, still times with God. However, we must not give up meeting with God in a still, quiet way. We know Jesus will take care of us. We will be healed. Notice what happens to Peter, James, and John in their moment of terror (See Matt: 17:6-7). Jesus came to them and touched them. You can imagine Jesus gently coming over to the disciples and bending down as Peter, James, and John are shaking in terror facedown on the ground. Jesus gently places his hand on them, touching them to soothe their fears. Jesus kindly and lovingly, with great compassion, tells them to not be afraid. They can get up; everything is going to be all right. Isn't it a comfort to know how much Jesus really cares about you? Isn't it such a waste of time to worry so much like we do? Jesus wants to take our fears away. He says, "Get up, and don't be afraid" (17:7).

If we can focus our eyes on Jesus, then we can see clearly and realize the peace we have with him. The disciples looked up and saw no one except Jesus. Let us look up and see only

Jesus. Jesus is all that we need. Let us meditate on him and be transformed by his Spirit.

> Our hearts were made for Thee, oh Lord,
> and restless will they ever be
> until at last we rest in Thee.
> St. Augustine

VI

An Out of This World Experience

13

Praying Intimately

Satan is Frightened!

This chapter was a struggle for me to write. I experienced mixed feelings for two nights in a row. I felt both a fearful foreboding and a calm peace. I had difficulty falling asleep, which is usually not a problem for me. Even now, as I am writing, I am not sure how to interpret these feelings. I wonder—has this chapter caught Satan's attention?

Satan always worries when we begin to pray and to draw closer to God. Satan is better pleased when we Christians simply go through the religious motions, having no real, true transforming relationship with our Almighty God. Satan does not want Christians to feel comfortable enough with God to call him Abba, Father, or "Daddy." He much prefers Christians to be so intimidated by the prospect of addressing God himself that they keep silent, not praying at all. There is a spiritual battle going on inside each one of us, and only God can give us peace, strength, and true comfort. Prayer is a key weapon in this warfare and a pathway to intimacy with God.

As I write, Satan is trying to distract me. Although I am worried and troubled in my heart and mind at this moment, God is telling me, "Do not be anxious about anything, [Anthony], but in everything, by prayer and petition, with thanksgiving, present your requests to me. And my peace, which transcends all understanding, will guard your heart and your mind in Christ Jesus" (Phil. 4:6-7). Satan is frightened! There is magnificent power in prayer!

Importance of Prayer

Nothing speaks more powerfully about the importance of prayer than the Bible's promises. The Scriptures promise the presence of God (Matt. 18:19-20), intimacy (Ps. 145:18), practical help (Matt. 21:22; 1 John 3:21-22), and profound spiritual growth (Jer. 33:3). A quick reading of the prayer verses at the end of the chapter will reactivate your appreciation for prayer.

The apostles and early Christians were clear on the need for continual prayer. Throughout the book of Acts, it was common practice for early Christians to be engaged in the simple and powerful act of prayer. When church-related activities threatened to take the apostles away from their devotional lives, they encouraged the young churches to delegate deacons to these activities so the apostles could "give [their] attention to prayer and the ministry of the Word" (Acts 6:4). The apostle Paul was a prayer warrior and spoke about prayer many times. In his letter to the Thessalonians, Paul encouraged its members to "pray continually" (1 Thess. 5:17). To the Romans, he wrote, "[Be] joyful in hope, patient in affliction, faithful in prayer" (Rom. 12:12).

During his life here on earth, Jesus himself took time from his important work of healing, feeding, teaching, and saving people in order to be refreshed and empowered by his Father through prayer.

Very early in the morning, while it was still dark, Jesus got up, left the house and went off to a solitary place, where he prayed. (Mark 1:35)

Even though Jesus was God, he still began his day in solitude and prayer with his Father and God before sunrise. Perhaps he understood that there is no better way to start the day than by going to God and communing with him. Early morning is such a peaceful time of the day; most people are still sleeping, the world seems so quiet, and it is the beginning of a new day. When we start the day as Jesus did in solitude and prayer, we are drawn closer to God for his strength, hope, love, and faith to help us through our day. God reminds us that he is with us no matter what happens and that he wants us to be close with him throughout the whole day. Remember when we come into his all-powerful, awesome presence, we are transformed into his likeness. When we go throughout the day and experience discouragement, disappointments, stress, frustrations, tragedies, rejections, loneliness, and hurt, we are reminded to come back to God's peaceful presence. He reminds us that he is our ultimate lover and friend who will never desert us (Matt. 28:20).

I find my day is more stressful when I neglect to start the day spending time with God in his word through prayer and meditation. However, for many of us, the daily distractions of home interfere with having a peaceful, quiet time with God. Even Jesus himself found it necessary at times to leave the house and go off to a solitary place where he prayed to his Father. Like Jesus, do you have a solitary place to go to every morning and pray? If not, could you get creative and make a special place for prayer early in your day? Do you have an enclosed porch or a family room or den that would be empty very early in the morning? What about the kitchen, before all of the activities begin? What about your finished basement or the children's play room?

More Than Technique

We need to realize that true and lasting transformation comes from God, not from ourselves. It is *not based on any techniques*; rather, it is us conforming to God and allowing his great power and presence to transform us. We just have to join him. "And we, who with unveiled faces all reflect the Lord's glory, are being transformed into his likeness with ever increasing glory, which comes from the Lord, who is the Spirit" (2 Cor. 3:18).

> The Biblical Christian can only pray empty-handed...Our hope depends not on the right technique or the proper phrase or gesture, which borders on magic, but on the promises of God...True prayer is neither mystical rapture nor ritual observance nor philosophical reflection: it is the outpouring of our soul before a living God, the crying to God 'out of the depths.'...One convicted of sin by the grace of God and moved to confession by the spirit of God can only utter such prayer. [1]

These amazing quotes show just how loving our God is, that he does not WANT any special, fancied-up communication with him. He just wants us, each of us to be who we truly are in our ugliness and beauty. Wouldn't you dress up to eat at the White House with the President, even if you didn't like him? In contrast, all God wants is for us to come in the way that we truly are. Nothing pleases him more than when we can cry with him, laugh with him, and share love.

Prayer is not some mechanical formula we perform to have good luck shine upon us, like some magical trickery. Prayer even goes beyond our own will and desires. I have not yet achieved a level of perfect union with God and don't think I ever will on this earth. However, there are times when

I am blessed with glimpses of a deeper closeness with God and the feeling that I am more aligned with his will. This happens at times when I am meditatively praying to God, resting in his presence. I may have my own prayer agenda and desires that I want God to fulfill, but what happens at times is that God's will and grace envelop my requests to where they become less important to me. It is a transforming, supernatural experience that God provides. He says that his peace transcends all understanding as we give all our concerns to him.

More Than Words

Prayer definitely goes beyond words, just as communication goes beyond words. We are always communicating with one another, through our words, thoughts, actions, behaviors, gestures, and spirit (See Rom. 8:26-27).

Prayer is a joining—a united connection with God. We are bonded, united, and fastened to God through Jesus Christ, who is the glue and bridge that makes and keeps this connection and communion with God possible and adhering. Only when we are joined to God by Jesus Christ and have this continual bond can we carry out the command to pray without ceasing (1 Thess. 5:17).

Communion means communication that includes direct, close relationship. It is the wordless communication between a mother and the baby who nurses at her breast—the close bond between the best of friends. The conversation between a man and woman deeply in love.[2]

True Prayer is for Lovers Only

We need to join God and have a love affair with him—to speak freely and intimately to God within the security of that love relationship. This is true prayer and how we become more intimate with God and hence transformed through him. "But when the kindness and love of God our Savior appeared, he saved us, not because of righteous things we had done, but because of his mercy. He saved us through the washing of rebirth and renewal by the Holy Spirit, whom he poured out on us generously through Jesus Christ our Savior" (Titus 3:4-6).

Prayer is the language used between two lovers, a language from the heart. "Real prayer comes not from gritting our teeth but from falling in love." [3]

The author C. Welton Gaddy wonderfully describes prayer:

As our love for God intensifies, our desire for contact with God grows. Then, the more contact we experience, the more we know about God, and the more profound our love becomes. Our love for God leads to communion with God. And our communion with God strengthens our love for God. The communion, which transpires within this love affair, is prayer. We find ourselves caught up in praying to God as a result of being in love with God. A life of prayer is a life of love, and vice versa. [4]

Let's not take this for granted and become like the Ephesian church who lost her first love (Rev. 2:4). For many of us, our love, zeal, and passion for Christ decrease over the years. Can you remember back to when you were baptized into Christ and the amount of love you had for him at that time? You were probably at the peak of your excitement for God. If you never felt a real loving passion for Christ or if you have lost that loving feeling, you can have that love rekindled. The key is to build a love relationship with God the same way you would with any other love in your life. Spend time together with him: times of speaking, times of listening, and times of silence.

We must be compelled by the love of Christ (2 Cor. 5:14), and "we love because he first loved us" (1 John. 4:19). God is the initiator, and we are the responders.

Prayer is our way to join with God in deep and abiding intimacy. Prayer allows us to feel God's presence with us always. This is why we are to pray without ceasing (1 Thess. 5:17). Our life is an unending prayer and communion with our Great Lover, God. I pray that God will always keep our eyes open to see him everywhere and at all times.

Practical Help

Prayer Promises

Let's take some time now to listen to God's promises for you now as you join him intimately in prayer and meditation on his words. You may want to use these passages as part of your daily quiet times, or meditate on only one of these Scriptures per day.

Before they call I will answer; while they are still speaking I will hear. (Isa. 65:24)

Therefore I tell you, whatever you ask for in prayer, believe that you have received it, and it will be yours. (Mark 11:24)

Ask and it will be given to you; seek and you will find; knock and the door will be opened to you. For everyone who asks receives; he who seeks finds; and to him who knocks, the door will be opened. (Matt. 7:7-8)

If you believe, you will receive whatever you ask for in prayer. (Matt. 21:22)

Again, I tell you that if two of you on earth agree about anything you ask for, it will be done for you by my Father in heaven. For where two or three come together in my name, there am I with them. (Matt. 18:19-20)

Dear friends, if our hearts do not condemn us, we have confidence before God and receive from him anything we ask, because we obey his commands and do what pleases him. (I John 3:21-22)

But when you pray, go into your room, close the door, and pray to your Father who is unseen. Then your Father, who sees what is done in secret, will reward you. (Matt. 6:6)

The LORD is near to all who call on him, to all who call on him in truth. (Ps. 145:18)

In that day you will no longer ask me anything. I tell you the truth, my Father will give you whatever you ask in my name. Until now you have not asked for anything in my name. Ask and you will receive, and your joy will be complete. (John 16:23-24)

Call to me and I will answer you and tell you great and unsearchable things you do not know. (Jer. 33:3)

He will call upon me, and I will answer him; I will be with him in trouble, I will deliver him and honor him. (Ps. 91:15)

The LORD is far from the wicked but he hears the prayer of the righteous. (Prov. 15:29)

Delight yourself in the LORD and he will give you the desires of your heart. (Ps. 37:4)

If you remain in me and my words remain in you, ask whatever you wish, and it will be given you. (John 15:7)

And I will do whatever you ask in my name, so that the Son may bring glory to the Father. You may ask me for anything in my name, and I will do it. (John 14:13-14)

I wait for you, O LORD; you will answer, O Lord my God. (Ps. 38:15)

If we confess our sins, he is faithful and just and will forgive us our sins and purify us from all unrighteousness. (1 John 1:9)

Very early in the morning, while it was still dark, Jesus got up, left the house and went off to a solitary place, where he prayed. (Mark 1:35)

And when you pray, do not be like the hypocrites, for they love to pray standing in the synagogues and on the street corners to be seen by men. I tell you the truth, they have received their reward in full. (Matt 6:5)

Do not be anxious about anything, but in everything, by prayer and petition, with thanksgiving, present your requests to God. And the peace of God, which transcends all understanding, will guard your hearts and your minds in Christ Jesus. (Phil. 4:6-7)

Is any one of you in trouble? He should pray. Is anyone happy? Let him sing songs of praise. Is any one of you sick? He should call the elders of the church to pray over him and anoint him with oil in the name of the Lord. And the prayer offered in faith will make the sick person well; the Lord will raise him up. If he has sinned, he will be forgiven. Therefore confess your sins to each other and pray for each other so that you may be healed. The prayer of a righteous man is powerful and effective. Elijah was a man just like us. He prayed earnestly that it would not rain, and it did not rain on the land for three and a half years. Again he prayed, and the heavens gave rain, and the earth produced its crops. (James 5:13-18)

This is the confidence we have in approaching God: that if we ask anything according to his will, he hears us. And if we know that he hears us—whatever we ask—we know that we have what we asked of him. (1 John. 5:14-15)

For the eyes of the Lord are on the righteous and his ears are attentive to their prayer; but the face of the Lord is against those who do evil. (1 Pet. 3:12)

Let us then approach the throne of grace with confidence, so that we may receive mercy and find grace to help us in our time of need. (Heb. 4:16)

If my people, who are called by my name, will humble themselves and pray and seek my face and turn from their wicked ways, then will I hear from heaven and will *forgive* their sin and will heal their land. (2 Chron. 7:14, emphasis mine)

Out of the depths I cry to you, O LORD; O Lord, hear my voice. Let your ears be attentive to my cry for mercy. (Ps. 130:1-2)

Hindrances to Prayer

It is also good to be aware of some hindrances to prayer and what could ultimately affect our intimate relationship with God.

Secret Sin - "If I had cherished sin in my heart, the Lord would not have listened" (Ps. 66:18).

Indifference - "Then they will call to me but I will not answer; they will look for me but will not find me. Since they hated knowledge and did not choose to fear the LORD, since they would not accept my advice and spurned my rebuke" (Prov. 1:29-30).

Neglect of Mercy - "If a man shuts his ears to the cry of the poor, he too will cry out and not be answered" (Prov. 21:13).

Despising the law (disobedience) - "If anyone turns a deaf ear to the law, even his prayers are detestable" (Prov. 28:9).

Bloodguiltiness - "When you spread out your hands in prayer, I will hide my eyes from you; even if you offer many prayers, I will not listen. Your hands are full of blood; wash and make yourselves clean. Take your evil deeds out of my sight! Stop doing wrong" (Isa. 1:15-16).

Iniquity - "But your iniquities have separated you from your God—your sins have hidden his face from you, so that he will not hear" (Isa. 59:2).
"Then they will cry out to the LORD, but he will not answer them. At that time he will hide his face from them because of the evil they have done" (Mic. 3:4).

Lying Lips - "But your iniquities have separated you from your God, your sins have hidden his face from you, so that he will not hear. For your hands are stained with blood, your fingers with guilt. Your lips have spoken lies, and your tongue mutters wicked things" (Isa. 59:2-3).

Stubbornness - "They made their hearts as hard as flint and would not listen to the law or to the words that the LORD Almighty had sent by his Spirit through the earlier prophets. So the LORD Almighty was very angry. 'When I called, they did not listen; so when they called, I would not listen,' says the LORD Almighty" (Zech. 7:12-13).

Instability - "He who doubts is like a wave of the sea, blown and tossed by the wind. That man should not think he will receive anything from the Lord—he is a double-minded man, unstable in all he does" (James 1:6-8).

Self-indulgence - "When you ask, you do not receive, because you ask with wrong motives, that you may spend what you get on your pleasures" (James 4:3).

Marital Discord - "They were submissive to their own husbands, like Sarah, who obeyed Abraham and called him her master. You are her daughters if you do what is right and do not give way to fear. Husbands, in the same way be considerate as you live with your wives, and treat them with respect as the weaker partner and as heirs with you of the gracious gift of life, so that nothing will hinder your prayers"(1 Pet. 3:5-7).

Conditions of Effective Prayer

True prayer is an encounter with the Holy in which we realize not only our creatureliness and guilt, but also the joy of knowing that our sins are forgiven through the atoning death of the divine Savior, Jesus Christ. In such an encounter, we are impelled not only to bow before God and seek his mercy, but also to offer thanksgiving for the grace that goes to undeserving sinners. [5]

Meaningful prayer is neither magical nor mechanical. It is personal and spiritual. Meaningful prayer is the honest talk that occurs between two lovers.

Contrition - "If my people, who are called by my name, will humble themselves and pray and seek my face and turn from their wicked ways, then will I hear from heaven and will forgive their sin and will heal their land" (2 Chron. 7:14).

Wholeheartedness - "'For I know the plans I have for you,' declares the LORD, 'plans to prosper you and not to harm you, plans to give you hope and a future. Then you will call upon me and come and pray to me, and I will listen to you. You will seek me and find me when you seek me with all your heart'" (Jer. 29:11-13).

Faith - "Have faith in God," Jesus answered. "I tell you the truth, if anyone says to this mountain, 'Go, throw yourself into the sea,' and does not doubt in his heart but believes that what he says will happen, it will be done for him. Therefore I tell you, whatever you ask for in prayer, believe that you have received it, and it will be yours" (Mark 11:22-24).

Righteousness - "Therefore confess your sins to each other and pray for each other so that you may be healed. The prayer of a righteous man is powerful and effective. Elijah was a man just like us" (James 5:16-17).

Obedience - "Dear friends, if our hearts do not condemn us, we have confidence before God and receive from him anything we ask, because we obey his commands and do what pleases him" (1 John 3:21-22).

"But I pray to you, O LORD, in the time of your favor; in your great love, O God, answer me with your sure salvation." (Ps. 69:13)

14

Fast and Focus

W hat's so important about fasting? Why did people fast throughout Biblical history, including the three greatest leaders: Moses, Elijah, and Jesus the Son of God? Why did these men fast for forty days and forty nights? What is the role of fasting in our spiritual transformation and in developing greater intimacy with God?

Why do people in various parts of the world fast even to the present day? Why have people practiced fasting for health reasons throughout time? What is it about fasting that makes it a universal practice in one form or another? What are the present-day benefits of fasting for us?

These are the questions we will answer in this chapter, along with some practical steps on how to fast.

First, a warning about fasting—fasting is not for everyone. Be sure you consult with your physician before you begin a fast. Fasting can be dangerous for people who have certain medical conditions such as diabetes, hypoglycemia, and kidney disease. According to James Balch, M.D. and Phyllis A. Balch, C.N.C., pregnant or lactating women should never fast.[1]

Fasting—what does it mean? Generally speaking, it means to abstain from food in some way. Biblical fasting refers to abstaining from food for spiritual purposes. The verb "fasting" comes from the Hebrew term *"tsum"* and the Greek word *"nesteia,"* which means to *"afflict soul or self"* (i.e. practice self-denial).[2]

Scholars differ on the origin of fasting. Some believe fasting was natural for the early people because they may have gone without food for days or weeks at a time, so fasting was therefore compulsory. Others believe the practice of fasting developed from the natural loss of appetite during times of sorrow and great distress. Fasting became an almost universal religious duty, which could have come from peoples' superstitious beliefs. "It was believed that the gods were jealous of the pleasures of men and that abstinence would propitiate their favor." [3] People have fasted throughout time for various reasons, including physical, emotional, and spiritual reasons.

All three fathers of western medicine, Hippocrates, Galen, and Paracelsus, concluded nearly 500 years ago that "fasting is the greatest remedy...the physician within!" Hippocrates also said, "Everyone has a doctor in him or her; we just have to help it in its work. The natural healing force within each one of us is the greatest force in getting well. Our food should be our medicine. Our medicine should be our food. But to eat when you are sick, is to feed your sickness."[4]

Dr. Joel Fuhrman said:

Fasting and natural diet, though essentially unknown [in today's United States] as a therapy, should be the first treatment when someone discovers that she or he has a medical problem. It should not be applied only to the most advanced cases, as is present practice. Whether the patient has a cardiac condition, hypertension, autoimmune disease, fibroids, or asthma, he or she must be informed that fasting and natural, plant-based diets are a viable alternative to conventional therapy, and an effective one. The time may come when *not* offering this substantially more effective nutritional approach will be considered malpractice.[5]

Fasting has been used for many physical and emotional concerns. Michael Murray and Joseph Pizzorno say:

Although therapeutic fasting is probably one of the oldest known therapies, the medical community, despite the fact that significant scientific research on fasting exists in the medical literature, has largely ignored it. Numerous medical journals have carried articles on the use of fasting in the treatment of obesity, chemical poisoning, rheumatoid arthritis, allergies, psoriasis, eczema, thrombophlebitis, leg ulcers, the irritable bowel syndrome, impaired or deranged appetite, bronchial asthma, depression, neurosis, and schizophrenia. [6]

Fasting helps detoxify the body of harmful toxins that tend to build up as a result of pollutants in the air, chemicals in our food and water, and in many other ways. These toxins and wastes in our system affect our health physically, emotionally, and spiritually. Therefore, more and more people today are rediscovering the many health benefits of fasting. However, the majority of people who fast these days do so for spiritual or religious reasons.

Let's concentrate now on biblically based fasting, for it is this type of fasting designed by God that is most effective for our true transformation and for becoming more intimate with God.

Biblical Fasting

Biblical fasting is deliberately abstaining from food for spiritual purposes. The focus is on God and is always accompanied with prayer. Biblical fasting is never done without prayer.

The Misuses of Biblical Fasting

Biblical fasting is not a physical or psychological discipline. In other words, its purpose is not for us to lose weight or to feel better about ourselves, although these are usually the side benefits of fasting. Biblical fasting is to attain spiritual goals. Many Christians testify to developing greater discipline from fasting on a regular basis. When you discipline yourself in your desire to eat, you become disciplined in other areas of your life as well. However, Biblical fasting is not solely for self-discipline. Fasting began to be misused by many of the monks and hermits in the fourth century.

Biblical fasting is also not a way to manipulate God, as many of the early religions believed. They thought that by fasting they could appease the gods and gain their sympathy.

Another misuse of fasting is what Jesus condemned: hypocritical fasting. The Pharisees fasted to be seen by men and they lost the true meaning of fasting.

True biblical fasting is a spiritual discipline used to help us become more open to God's will and his control, not the other way around. Fasting helps us to slow down and to become more humble. When we become physically weak, we can become more spiritually in tune to God if we focus on him. We become more sensitive to hearing God.

Various Types of Biblical Fasts

There are four types of fasts, three of which are mentioned in the Bible.

1. The *normal fast* is abstaining from food but not water. The duration of this fast can vary. It can be one day, as in Judges 20:26. "Then the Israelites, and all the people, went up to Bethel, and there they sat weeping before the Lord. They fasted that day until evening and presented burnt offerings and fellowship offerings to the Lord." Jesus experienced a normal fast, which lasted 40 days and nights (Matt. 4:1-2; Mark 1:12-13; Luke 4:1-2).

2. The *absolute fast* is abstaining from food and water. A human being cannot usually live beyond three days without water. The absolute fast of Moses for 40 days and 40 nights (Deut. 9:9,18) was a miraculous fast because he had neither food nor water. Other examples of the absolute fast are Elijah (1 Kings 19:8), Ezra (Ezra 10:6), Esther and her household (Esther 4:16), and Paul (Acts 9:9).

3. The *partial fast* is restriction of certain foods or abstaining from one meal a day. A partial fast may consist of eating only vegetables, as in the case of Daniel, Shadrach, Meshach, and Abednego, who only ate vegetables and drank water (Dan. 10:3).

4. The *rotational fast* is abstaining or eating certain families of food for designated periods. For example, meat may be eaten every day except Fridays. Other families of food may be omitted from one's diet on other days. This type of fast is not found in the Bible.

The Spiritual Purpose of Biblical Fasting

We see various spiritual purposes for Biblical fasting, but all were focused on God and his relationship with his people.

There were numerous occasions in the Bible when people fasted, such as:

Mourning someone's death

"When the people of Jabesh Gilead heard of what the Philistines had done to Saul, all of their valiant men journeyed through the night to Beth Shan. They took down the bodies of Saul and his sons from the wall of Beth Shan and went to Jabesh, where they burned them. Then they took their bones and buried them under a tamarisk tree at Jabesh and *they fasted seven days.*" (1 Sam 31:11-13, emphasis mine)

Even David and his men fasted for Saul. "Then David and all the men with him took hold of their clothes and tore them. They *mourned and wept and fasted* till evening for Saul and his son Jonathan, and for the army of the Lord and the house of Israel, because they had fallen by the sword" (2 Sam. 1:12; 3:35, emphasis mine).

Mourning sin

When Moses returned with the original tablets of stone he was deeply sorrowful about the sin of the people.

"Then once again I fell prostrate before the Lord for forty days and forty nights; *I ate no bread and drank no water*, because of all the sin you had committed, doing what was evil in the Lord's sight and so provoking him to anger" (Deut. 9:18, emphasis mine).

Other occasions include the Israelites assembled at Mizpah, fasting and confessing their sin before the Lord (1 Sam. 7:6), the admission of Ahab's sin (1 Kings 21:27), mourning for the nation of Israel while they were in exile (Ezra 10:6), the entire city of Nineveh after hearing the words of Jonah (Jon. 3:5), and the three-day fast of Saul after being struck on the road to Damascus (Acts 9:3-9).

Impending danger and need for protection

"There, by the Ahava Canal, *I proclaimed a fast*, so that we might humble ourselves before our God and ask him for a safe journey for us and our children, with all our possessions. I was ashamed to ask the king for soldiers and horsemen to protect us from enemies on the road, because we had told the king, the gracious hand of our God is on everyone who looks to him, but his great anger is against all who forsake him. So we *fasted and petitioned* our God about this, and he answered our prayer. On the twelfth day of the first month we set out from the Ahava Canal to go to Jerusalem. The hand of our God was on us, and he protected us from enemies and bandits along the way. So we arrived in Jerusalem, where we rested three days." (Ezra 8:21, 23, 31, 32, emphasis mine)

Other examples are found in Jeremiah 36:9 and Esther 4:3.

For direction

"After this, the Moabites and Ammonites with some of the Meunites came to make war on Jehoshaphat. Some men came and told Jehoshaphat, 'A vast army is coming against you from Edom, from the other side of the sea. It is already in Hazazon Tamar' (that is, En Gedi). Alarmed, Jehoshaphat resolved to inquire of the Lord, and *he proclaimed a fast* for all Judah. The people of Judah came together to seek help from the Lord;

indeed, they came from every town in Judah to seek him" (2 Chron. 20:1-4, emphasis mine).

The account goes on to say that because of the faith the people of Judah had in God, he arranged for the three enemies of Judah to destroy one another. The armies of Jehoshaphat didn't have to conduct one battle. They merely carried off the plunder left behind by their now destroyed enemies.

On behalf of someone who is sick

David fasted on behalf of his son born through Bathsheba.

"After Nathan had gone home, the Lord struck the child that Uriah's wife had borne to David, and he became ill. David pleaded with God for the child. He *fasted* and went into his house and spent the nights lying on the ground. The elders of his household stood beside him to get him up from the ground, but he refused, and he *would not eat any food* with them." (2 Sam. 12:15-17, emphasis mine)

"Yet when they were ill, I put on sackcloth and *humbled myself with fasting.* When my prayers returned to me unanswered, I went about mourning as though for my friend or brother." (Ps. 35:13-14, emphasis mine)

The appointment of missionaries or church leaders

"Paul and Barnabas appointed elders for them in each church and, *with prayer and fasting*, committed them to the Lord, in whom they had put their trust." (Acts 14:23, emphasis mine)

"While they were worshiping the Lord and *fasting*, the Holy Spirit said, 'Set apart for me Barnabas and Saul for the work to which I have called them'" (Acts 13:2, emphasis mine).

For special revelation

"I, Daniel, understood from the Scriptures, according to the word of the Lord given to Jeremiah the prophet, that the desolation of Jerusalem would last seventy years. So I turned to the Lord God and pleaded with him in prayer and petition, *in fasting* and in sackcloth and ashes...Now, our God, hear the prayers and petitions of your servant. For your sake, O Lord, look with favor on your desolate sanctuary. Give ear, O God, and hear; open your eyes and see the desolation of the city that bears your Name. We do not make requests of you because we are righteous but because of your great mercy. O Lord, listen! O Lord, forgive! O Lord, hear and act! For your sake, O my God, do not delay, because your city and your people bear your Name." (Dan. 9:2-3, 17-19, emphasis mine)

In humiliation

"On the twenty-fourth day of the same month, the Israelites gathered together, *fasting* and wearing sackcloth and having dust on their heads. Those of Israelite descent had separated themselves from all foreigners. They stood in their places and confessed their sins and the wickedness of their fathers. They stood where they were and read from the Book of the Law of the Lord their God for a quarter of the day, and spent another quarter in confession and in worshiping the Lord their God." (Neh. 9:1-3, emphasis mine)

Fasting of Biblical People

We see many examples in the Bible of people who fasted on a regular basis:

John the Baptist's disciples

"Then John's disciples came and asked him, 'How is it that we and the Pharisees *fast*, but your disciples do not fast?'"(Matt. 9:14, emphasis mine)

Anna

"She never left the temple but worshiped night and day, *fasting* and praying." (Luke. 2:37, emphasis mine)

The Pharisees (albeit hypocritically)

"I *fast* twice a week and give a tenth of all I get." (Luke. 18:12, emphasis mine)

Paul

"I have labored and toiled and have often gone without sleep; I have known hunger and thirst and have *often gone without food*; I have been cold and naked." (2 Cor. 11:27, emphasis mine)

There are numerous examples, reasons, and types of fasts in the Bible. For a more detailed presentation of fasting in the Bible, see *Fasting for Spiritual Breakthrough,* by Elmer Towns.[7]

Although we have explored examples of fasting—along with how it can be misused—fasting is not a command for Christians. Jesus did not say "if" you fast, or "you must" fast, but rather "*when*" you fast (Matt. 6:16,17). Jesus assumed Christians would continue to fast. He also said that his disciples would fast when he departed from this earth (Matt. 9:15). Fasting appears to be a spiritual discipline needed for a more intimate walk with God (Acts 13:2).

However, biblical fasting is a very neglected spiritual discipline among most Christians. We need to get back to this vital discipline to draw closer to God. We have been conditioned to indulge ourselves, which opposes the concept of fasting. It is important to occasionally fast so we can humble ourselves before God and enter into a deeper closeness to him. Fasting will help us to go beyond the superficialities of our life and focus on the spiritual desires of God. The early church viewed fasting with great spiritual importance and we need to get back to the practice of fasting.

Fasting is, however, voluntary. It is not meant to be obligatory, as some religious groups require today. Fasting became an essential part of life for asceticism in post-apostolic times, which led to several interpolations in the scriptures of the word fasting. In Matthew 17:21; Mark 9:29; Acts 10:30, and 1 Corinthians 7:5, the word *fasting* was added to later Bible manuscripts. Some of the more reliable manuscripts such as the Sinaiticus and Vaticanus omit Matt. 17:21 and the word "fasting" from Mark 9:29. Those two manuscripts and the Alexandrinus manuscript omit "fasting and" from 1 Corinthians 7:5. Even though people tried to impress the importance of fasting, we cannot command people to do it. You must be willing to fast, which comes from your heart to draw closer to God.

A word of caution—let's not become like the ascetic monks and Pharisees, who prescribed certain set times for fasting. The Pharisees fasted on Tuesdays and Thursdays, while the early church fasted on Wednesdays and Fridays. Fasting must be a voluntary act of submission to God for the purpose of focusing on him. Before entering any fast, we need to prepare ourselves spiritually, mentally, and emotionally.

Fasting Preparation

Spiritually

Determine your motives, reasons, and purposes for fasting. Ask yourself if your purpose is to draw nearer to God for his glory to be revealed, then examine your heart and confess your sins to the Lord. Plan how you might use your time of fasting to focus on God and his will. Do much praying and Bible reading during your fast.

Mentally

Preparing your mind is important for spiritual as well as physical reasons. Weigh the purpose for your fast, the benefits you anticipate, the struggles you may encounter, and the outcome you expect. The outcome you desire should be what God desires for you and should be on his terms.

I remember prior to and throughout my two-week survival course how the instructors constantly reminded us that the worst part of getting through the adventure was more mental than physical. Although hard to believe, our experience proved it true. God has given us a powerful mind to use for his glory—be open to him.

Physically

Fasting is a spiritual discipline, which requires physical participation. First, consult with your physician to see if you are physically able to fast. Physical preparation for fasting includes easing into it gradually and once it is completed, breaking the fast gradually. Before you start a fast, particularly extended fasts, you should eat smaller meals before you abstain totally. Do not have a big feast before your fast. Wean yourself off caffeine and sugar products.

Fasting Designed by God

I believe God designed and created us for his glory and purpose, and I believe fasting is an opportunity for us humans to experience another facet of life as designed by God. Each of us has been created with a sense of eternity deep within us (Eccles. 3:11). Our life's challenge is to learn to recognize the constant reminders of the sovereignty of God and our dependence on him. When we go without food, we become physically weak; however, our spiritual senses become heightened. This process can lead us to a greater appreciation of our need for God and for how he provides for us.

If you have ever had the stomach flu, or if you have ever felt depressed or stressed over a particular situation in your life, you may have experienced a loss of appetite. You just didn't feel like eating anything. This loss of appetite could be viewed as a "natural" way to fast. Perhaps a better view would be a God-given opportunity to become more aware of his supreme power and to draw closer to him.

The science and natural world look at fasting from a physiological perspective and see it as a natural and needed practice for the human body to recuperate and heal itself. As discussed above, Hippocrates, the father of Western medicine, believed that "everyone has a doctor in him or her; we just have to help it in its work."

God, however, had a greater plan for the "natural" process of fasting. It was not just for us to be physically healthy and to live longer on earth; fasting is designed to point us to the one who provides for all our needs. It helps refocus our attention on what really matters in life—a relationship with God.

Many things distract us from our relationship with God. Sometimes the desires of our hearts and our life's ambitions hinder us from having a pure heart toward God. Our pride and defenses get in the way of an open honest relationship with our true love, God. It is this false self that we need to rid from ourselves and to allow our true self to come before God for his mercy, grace, and love; only then will we feel his acceptance, forgiveness, and love; only then will we feel and experience God's love and transforming power; only then will we become more intimate with our God who first loved us.

I strongly believe that through fasting and prayer to God, we will be more open to allow God to work with us, in us, and through us. Fasting is a way to strip down our sinful defenses of pride, self-righteousness, greed, lust, and desires to control our false self.

My Desert Fasting

As I shared with you earlier in the book, I spent two weeks in the desert on a survival mission with little food and water. Along with our guides, we hiked for miles deep into the desert. To say that we were exhausted at the end of our quest, understates our experience. I became weakened physically. My body and mind slowed down. During that time, my pride was diminished, and many trivial things in my life no longer mattered. It did not bother me that I had not showered or shaved in days, nor did it bother me to not have any toilet paper for the entire two-week period.

What did matter was caring for one another in the group and helping one another through each of our various hardships and sufferings during that time. When our mouths were parched while hiking in the hot sun and only a few sips of water remained in the cup we were carrying, we didn't hesitate to give it to the one who needed it the most, the one who was faint and weak. We supported, helped, and sympathized with each other. We were able to overlook little annoyances that would have been more upsetting at other times—like how we looked or smelled.

This survival course was a spiritual awakening for me. It helped me to learn to rely on God more fully. The experience allowed my true self to come out; I just wanted to survive. Three of the fourteen days were spent solo. I was alone, on my own, somewhere in the mountains of Utah. I alone was responsible for building my own shelter in order to keep dry and somewhat protected from the rain while sleeping on the ground. I had no sleeping bag or tent. I had no food to eat mainly because I could not get a fire started. I had no access to matches, lighters, or propane gas starters, and because of the rain, could not get a fire started by rubbing wood together. In addition to having no matches, we also had no flashlights, no watches, and no comforts of modern-day convenience.

I was able to get water from a stream nearby my campsite, and that was a lifesaver. I spent the entire time fasting and praying. It was a spiritual time, teaching me to be still and to wait patiently for the Lord. Aside from building my shelter out of tree branches, tree bark, and leaves, I had nothing else to do. As long as it was daylight, I spent time reading the Bible. At all times I prayed. Like Elijah, I kept waiting for a powerful earth-shaking transformation to take place during this time. However, again like Elijah, God spoke to me in a whisper, constantly reminding me that "my grace is sufficient for you, for my power is made perfect in weakness" (2 Cor.

12:9). I developed a greater appreciation of God's all-sufficient grace and power during this solo time.

Because fasting can be a transforming experience, let me once again reiterate that the main point of fasting is for the purposes of God. It is an individual decision and a voluntary act of spiritual worship to God. Fasting is a spiritual discipline that is always joined with prayer. It is a way to humble us before God and submit to his will for our lives. Again, it appears that Jesus assumed Christians would fast, but it was not commanded or rejected. He strongly cautioned us against fasting for the wrong reason or motives (See Matt. 6:16-18).

Fasting, prayer, and solitude are ways to still our body and our mind to allow God to stir up our soul with his Holy Spirit. These are ways to quiet the distractions of the world and Satan. These are ways we can be more open and receptive to hearing God and obeying him. We are more able to then allow God to transform us into his likeness. Jesus himself said, "If anyone would come after me, he must deny himself and take up his cross and follow me. For whoever wants to save his life will lose it, but whoever loses his life for me will find it" (Matt. 16:24-25; Luke 9:23. See also Matt. 10:37-39 and Luke 14:26-27).

Fasting, prayer, and solitude also help us to be more receptive to God's Word. We are then more ready and willing to allow his word to transform our minds. We will become less interested in being conformed by the world (Rom. 12:1-2). Our confidence will come from the transforming power of God through his word and Spirit. How will you prepare yourself to hear God and obey him?

"Even now," declares the LORD, "return to me with all your heart, with fasting, weeping and mourning." (Joel 2:12)

15

The Penetrating Word

As we are being transformed, we must make sure we are being transformed into God's image and not our own or the world's. We are continually bombarded by ungodly influences of society and the world. We are overloaded with sources of information and communication through the media, over the Internet, from Hollywood, even through our government and the people with whom we associate. Not all of this information is bad; however, most of it is not from the mind of God. Satan's influences that are contrary to God's ways continually contaminate our thinking, seducing us into believing ourselves to be our own gods.

As mentioned in the beginning of this book, many people are desperately searching for some type of transformation. Most are seeking transformation by their own means, trying harder and harder to find meaning and joy in their lives. Because many of these attempts at transformation are manmade, they are short lived and without everlasting hope—but this is not something new to man. This search for a new life with new meaning and joy is as old as Adam and Eve. From the moment they turned away from God to follow their own appetite, they fell away from the perfect relationship with God in the Garden of Eden. They believed the lies of Satan. It was the beginning of the search for completion, seeking, and being fooled by the philosophies of man. As present in the Garden as it was present during the days of Jesus, so it is present in our lives today.

The apostle Paul sums it up very well:

> See to it that no one takes you captive through hollow and deceptive philosophy, which depends on human tradition and the basic principles of this world rather than on Christ. (Col. 2:8)

If we really want to be transformed and have greater intimacy with God, we need to be guided by his word and not the world's word. Think of it this way: in order for our automobile's engine to run smoothly, we need to regularly change the oil. If we ignore this practice, the oil will eventually become so contaminated and weak that our engine will overheat and stop working.

Similarly, our minds need constant changing and cleaning. Because our faith actually comes from the Word of Christ (Rom. 10:17), we need to let the Word of God dwell in us richly (Col. 3:16). When we abide in the Word of God daily through daily Bible study and meditation, our faith is transformed and grows deeper. The Bible helps us clean our minds by revealing to us the things to think about "...whatever is noble, whatever is right, whatever is pure, whatever is lovely, whatever is admirable, and whatever is excellent or praiseworthy..." (Phil. 4:8). We need to continually cleanse our minds with God's Word.

Although the Bible is the largest-selling book in the world, it is the least read. For many Christians, taking or making the time to study God's Word is a major problem. Although many of us take the availability of the Bible for granted, countless thousands of others around the world would gladly give all they have for the opportunity to read a Bible.

Perhaps many of us don't realize that over two thousand years, people have lost their lives struggling to ensure that future generations would be able to read the Bible in their own language (people are still losing their lives over this, e.g. China). Some of the first translators of the Bible into English were excommunicated from the church (Wyclif's Bible, A.D. 1382) and ordered by the governing authorities to be burned alive at the stake. (Tyndale's Bible A.D.1525, Tyndale burned to death on Oct. 6, 1536).

In the fifteenth century, a man named John Gutenberg (A.D. 1454) found a better way to make the holy Word of God accessible to everyone by inventing the printing press. Using the printing press meant that Bibles were reproduced at a less costly price, in a more timely fashion, and in greater quantities. Previously, Bibles cost a year's wages and took months, even years, to complete because they were all hand copied.

Even in our own country, the main purpose of early public education was to teach the masses how to read and write so that they could read and study the Bible. How far we have come from our appreciation and respect for the Word of God!

Despite the continuous persecution the Bible has suffered throughout its rich history, the Word of God has always prevailed, for the Word of God is eternal and can never be destroyed. Human philosophies and laws come and go, but the Word of God is forevermore.

It is essential for a child of God to read the Word of God daily—for we cannot live or survive spiritually without it. Through it we are reminded in various ways how God gives us life through his word. We are told by God in Deuteronomy 8:3 that he humbled the Israelites by causing them to hunger and then fed them manna while wandering in the desert for forty years. This was to help the Israelites become dependent on God and not their own ingenuity in order to survive. God says he did this to teach them that "man does not live by bread alone but on every word that comes from the mouth of the Lord" (Deut. 8:3).

Jesus later quoted this verse to Satan who tried to tempt him in his desert experience (Matt. 4:4). Jesus was emphasizing the same principle—that our sustenance must come from God who loves us, and unless we have the spiritual food, which comes from God, we cannot have a healthy relationship with the One who is the Word.

When we realize the power of God's Word, the Bible, we can have a greater appreciation for the Word. We realize the Word is God in the flesh, even Jesus Christ:

In the beginning was the Word and the Word was with God, and the Word was God. He was with God in the beginning. (John 1:1-2)

The Word became flesh and made his dwelling among us. We have seen his glory, the glory of the One and Only, who came from the Father, full of grace and truth. (John 1:14)

This "Word of God" means God himself, and he came to us in a physical form on this earth as Jesus Christ, the Son of God. The Word existed in the beginning of all time, and the Word will last for all time. Jesus himself said, "Heaven and earth will pass away, but my words will never pass away" (Matt. 24:35). The Word of God is powerful because it is God, and it is eternal.

Contrary to some beliefs, the Bible did not originate from man. No prophecy or proclamation of Scripture came from the will of man or from his own understanding, but the Bible came from God who spoke through men by the Holy Spirit (1 Peter 1:20-21).

God's Word, the Bible, comes from the mind of God, and his thoughts are very different from our thoughts and ways. God says, "For my thoughts are not your thoughts, neither are your ways my ways. As the heavens are higher than the earth, so are my ways higher than your ways and my thoughts than your thoughts" (Isa. 55:8-9).

Therefore, when we read the Bible, we are reading the mind of God himself. The Word we read is Jesus Christ himself who is God (See John 1:1-2,14). This makes the Bible an actual, living word that is active and powerful. "For the Word of God is living and active..." (Heb. 4:12). The Bible is able to penetrate both our soul and spirit. God's Word is active in accomplishing his purposes of redemption, salvation, and transformation.

It was by God's Word that the heavens existed in the first place, and that the earth was formed out of water and by water (2 Pet. 3:5). God just spoke the word, and it was done. God is true to his powerful word because God is his Word (John 1:1). The Word is Jesus Christ the Son of God. The Word came to man by the Holy Spirit of God (1 Peter 1:20-21). The Father, Son, and Holy Spirit are alive, powerful, and active just as God's Word says. God's Word cannot be taken lightly nor neglected if we want to be transformed and saved, for it is the power for salvation to all who believe and obey it.

The apostle Paul said that he was not ashamed of the gospel (the good news), "...because it is the power of God for salvation to everyone who believes" (Rom. 1:16). If you believe God's Word and obey it, you will be transformed into a child of God. This can only come from God himself if you allow him to do his part on his terms.

Perhaps the main reason for our neglect of God's Word is because we, as with Martha in Luke 10, allow everyday tasks to distract us. And unlike Mary, who made time to listen to the Word of God, we become stimulated and enticed by the many noises that drown out the gentle whisper of God.

In Mark 4:14ff, Jesus compares God's Word to that of a farmer who sowed his seed. The seed, of course, being the Word of God, sown throughout the end of time. Jesus used this illustration to show four different reactions people have to God's Word.

> The farmer plants the Word. Some people are like the seed that falls on the hardened soil of the road. No sooner do they hear the Word than Satan snatches away what has been planted in them. And some are like the seed that lands in the gravel. When they first hear the Word, they respond with great enthusiasm. But there is such shallow soil of character that when the emotions wear off and some difficulty arrives, there is nothing to show for it. The seed cast in the weeds represents the ones who hear the kingdom news but are overwhelmed with worries about all the things they have to do and all the things they want to get. The stress strangles what they heard, and nothing comes of it. But the seed planted in the good earth represents those who hear the Word, embrace it, and produce a harvest beyond their wildest dreams. (Mark 4:14-20 MSG)

In summary, the Bible is God's love letter to his children. God is powerful. If we allow it, the Word of God will transform us, but we must be willing to let him in. To be transformed, we need to allow his presence, power, and love to overtake us.

When we take time to know God personally, passionately, and powerfully, we will fall deeply in love with him and his Word to follow and obey.

Do not conform any longer to the pattern
of the world, but be transformed by
the renewing of your mind.
(Rom. 12:2)

Epilogue

To know Christ! What greater goal in life is there? Focusing on Christ in all we do and in all our situations will help us achieve this great goal. Paul says, "I want to know Christ" (Phil. 3:10). Jesus says the greatest commandment is to love God (Matt. 22:37). The writer of Ecclesiastes states, "Now all has been heard; here is the conclusion of the matter: Fear God and keep his commandments, for this is the whole [duty] of man" (Eccles. 12:13).

Therefore, the most important aspect of our transformation is our relationship with God. The bottom line is that we must love God first and foremost. If we do this, the rest will follow. In order to love God, we must develop a deep, personal, and intimate relationship with him, and the key to intimacy is to spend time with him.

My goal of this book was to teach you how to become intimate with God and allow him to transform you into his likeness (2 Cor. 3:18). I hope that you will take the necessary time to practice these spiritual disciplines described in this book. There is no shortcut or quick fix in becoming intimate with God. I hope you will continue to practice meditating on God every day and be blessed by his loving grace.

Appendix:

DISCUSSION QUESTIONS

Introduction

1. Rate your life on a scale from one to ten on how busy you are with ten being extremely busy and one being much time for quiet time.

    1   2   3   4   5   6   7   8   9   10

2. When was the last time you sat still in the presence of God focusing on him, putting aside everything else? How long did you spend the still time with God? What did you experience during this quiet time with God?

3. Describe the type of spiritual "blahs" you experience at times. Do you feel disconnected from God? Do you feel he is not there for you? Do you find it difficult to read the Bible and pray?

4. What happens when you are spiritually weak? In what ways do you tend to fill that emptiness or sense of loneliness?

5. What do you think the outcome will be when you apply the principles of this book to your life?

6. Describe the type of spiritual life with God you want.

7. What will you do to achieve the spiritual life you want?

Chapter 1: God Transformed My Switchblade Into a Sword

1. Are there areas in your life God has transformed? If so, describe what they are.

2. How can God transform your life?

3. Are there areas in your life that still need to be transformed into the image of God? Are these areas of your life that you have not yet fully turned over and yielded to God?

4. How do you feel that your life will be transformed by spending more personal, quiet time with God?

5. What practical ways will you start to draw more intimate with God for him to transform you into his image?

Chapter 2: What Is God's Passion?

1. In what ways do you think you might be neglecting your relationship with God? What is lacking? What do you spend most of your time doing?

2. How can we fool ourselves into thinking we are close to God or pleasing to him?

3. How can you fulfill the first and second Greatest Commandment?

4. How do we achieve greater intimacy with God and with others?

5. Why do you think you do not spend more time just with you and God alone?

6. How can you tell if someone is loosing interest in you? Or drifting away from you? In what ways do we reveal a decrease or drifting away from God?

Chapter 3: Biblical Meditation

1. What is biblical meditation and how does it differ from New Age and Eastern religion forms of meditation?

2. Why does God want us to meditate on him and how does that draw us closer to God?

3. How should we meditate according to the Bible?

4. Why did Jesus often go away to a solitary place to pray and meditate on God?

5. What are the many benefits of Christian meditation?

6. How will you begin your journey closer to God through biblical meditation?

Chapter 4: Are You a Martha or a Mary?

1. Rate yourself on a scale from one to ten on how well you listen to others with one being very weak to ten being a very attentive-active listener.

    1   2   3   4   5   6   7   8   9   10

    Now ask someone who knows you well or intimately to rate you on how well he or she thinks you listen. Tell him or her to be honest and that you won't get upset with him/her. This is a very important skill for intimacy. Do you need to improve your listening skills?

2. What distracts you from listening? –Things, other thoughts, time, personal problems…?

3. If you are not a good listener with others—how well of a listener do you think you are with God?

4. How can you improve your listening skills?

5. Describe in what ways you are a Martha at times and a Mary at times.

6. What are some practical ways you can meditate on God to be more in tune with him?

7. When will you start taking the time God gives to you to meditate on him?

Chapter 5: A Mountaintop Experience

1. Have you ever had a mountaintop experience? Explain what it was and how you felt from the experience.

2. What kind of effect did this mountaintop experience have on your life and how long has it affected you?

3. What would be your response if you were in a park and all of a sudden, you saw Moses, Elijah, and Jesus? How attentive would you be to listen to and heed what they said to you?

4. Have you ever had a quiet meditative time when you felt more in tune with God and moved by his presence?

    a. If not, what can help you experience God in a deeper way?
    b. How did Peter "fall into a trance" (Acts 10:10) and what resulted after this experience with God?

5. Where, when, and how can you have a meditative, quiet time with Jesus in solitude?

    a. What effects do you think this will have on your life?

Chapter 6: Moses Meets God Face to Face

1.   Describe a time when you felt weary and worn out wondering where God was?

    a. What were your complaints to God during this time when you felt he was not hearing you or answering your prayers? How did you feel?

2.   What are we to realize and do when we grow impatient or unaware of God's response to us?

3.   How can we prepare ourselves to meet God?

4.   How can we continually allow the radiance of Christ to shine through us?

5.   Why is being still before God in a place of solitude so difficult for many, including us, at times?

6.   What can you do to be more in tune with God and more receptive to his convicting and healing Word?

Chapter 7: Elijah Hears the Gentle Whisper

1.   Have you ever felt so worn out and discouraged to the point of depression? Can you relate to Elijah?

    a. How did you respond to such a time?

2.   How can our times of feeling weak and helpless help us in our intimacy with God and lead to a greater transformation?

3.   What are some "survival courses" life has brought you?

      a. How did you survive?
      b. Looking back, can you now see how God was preparing you for greater things for his glory?

4.   How can we look at and deal with our future "survival courses?"

5.   How can we be transformed by God?

6.   What gets in our way of trusting God and waiting patiently for him?

7.   What would help us to trust God more and obey him with patience?

8.   How will you put to use the practical applications in this book?

Chapter 8: Jesus Hears His Father's Voice

1.   What things/activities in your life make you feel too busy to stop, take time out, and just be still in the presence of God?

2.   How important or essential are these time-consuming things/activities in your life in view of eternity? How will you view these things/activities if you were to look at them from

heaven? How much would they really matter compared to having built a deeper relationship with God and others? (Matt. 22:36-37)

3.   How did Jesus prepare himself for his ministry?

4.   What did Moses, Elijah, and Jesus have in common? Who were the three on the Mount of Transfiguration?

5.   Explain why Jesus spent 40 days and 40 nights in the desert in solitude and fasting?

6.   In what ways is Jesus like us?

7.   How did Jesus find continual renewal?

8.   What practical things will you do to find continual renewal, strength, and peace with God?

Chapter 9: How To Be Still Physically

1.   How are you doing physically? How many stress-exhaustion physical symptoms can you check in the list?

2.   What do you usually do to deal with these physical symptoms?

3.   What do you do when you start to feel tired with less energy during the day?

4.   What are the reasons why you don't stop and take time out for yourself to just sit and relax?

5. How do you think you can benefit from responding to your ultradian troughs as described in this chapter?

6. What practical and feasible things can you do during your ultradian troughs in order to allow yourself to be renewed?

Chapter 10: How To Be Still Emotionally

1. How are you doing emotionally, mentally, and in your relationships with others? How many symptoms do you have from the lists in this chapter?

2. How do you usually deal with your uncomfortable emotions? What escape or vise do you use to dull or avoid the pain?

3. What is the outcome usually of your attempted solutions to your emotional issues or pain?

4. What new ways can you receive true healing and freedom as described in this chapter?

5. What are some new ways you plan to practice in your life to draw closer to God and be transformed into his likeness?

Chapter 11: How To Be Still Spiritually

1.   How are you doing spiritually? How many spiritual stress symptoms do you have as described in this chapter?

2.   What do you do when you experience any of these spiritual stress symptoms?

3.   How do you try to make yourself feel better spiritually?

4.   What are some ways we can become more humble and dependent on God rather than on things?

5.   What are some practical principles you have learned so far that can help you to be more of your true self before God and others?

Chapter 12: Transformation Results

1.   Describe the fourfold process of transformation.

2.   Have you ever experienced any of these four stages of transformation? Describe your experience? How did that experience come about?

3.   Have you ever been afraid or felt uncomfortable with approaching God face to face? Describe your experience.

4.   When was the last time you fell to your knees in desperation to God? Describe your experience.

5.   What can you do to feel more confident to approach the throne of God?

Chapter 13: Praying Intimately

1. How is your prayer life?

2. How do you think your prayer life is affected by your relationship with God?

3. How can your prayer life and hence relationship with God be improved?

4. What stands out the most to you from the Scriptures in this chapter about prayer, and why?

5. What will you do differently to improve your relationship and prayer life with God?

Chapter 14: Fast and Focus

1. What comes to your mind when you think of fasting?

2. What were some of the different beliefs of the origin of fasting?

3. What are some of the proposed medical and health benefits of fasting?

4. What distinguishes biblical fasting from other types of fasting?

5. Describe the four types of fasting—three of which are in the Bible.

6. What are some of the reasons for fasting found in the Bible?

7. Did Jesus assume Christians would continue to fast?

8. Why do you think Christians neglect the spiritual discipline of fasting so much?

Chapter 15: The Penetrating Word

1. In what ways might our society and the world influence us?

2. How can we recondition and cleanse our minds to be more like the mind of God?

3. What are some of the sacrifices people made in order for us to be able to read the Bible for ourselves?

4. Describe several attributes of God's Word.

5. How will you adjust your time and study with God's Word?

Notes

Introduction

1. David Kopp, Heather Harpham Kopp, and Larry Wilson, eds., *Praying for the World's 365 Most Influential People* (Eugene, Oregon: Harvest House Publishers, 1999), 257.

Part I—The Key to Transformation

Chapter 1: God Transformed My Switchblade Into a Sword

May you be transformed into God's likeness on a daily basis and your life be filled with his rich blessings.

Part II—Do You Hear the Bridegroom Calling?

Chapter 2: What Is God's Passion?

"Love the Lord your God with all your heart and with all your soul and with all your mind. And the second is like it: Love your neighbor as yourself. All the Law and the prophets hang on these two commandments." (Matt. 22:37-40)

Chapter 3: Biblical Meditation

1. Richard Foster, *Celebration of Discipline* (San Francisco: Harper & Row, 1978), 15.
2. ibid.
3. ibid.
4. Towns, L. Elmer, *Biblical Meditation for Spiritual Breakthrough* (Ventura, Calif.: Regal, 1998), 22.

Chapter 4: Are You a Martha or a Mary? The Importance of Listening

Jesus says, "Heaven and earth will pass away, but my words will never pass away." (Matt. 24:35)

Part III—From the Mountaintop to the Rooftop

Chapter 5: A Mountaintop Experience

Where can you go to be alone,
away from people, phones, and faxes?

Chapter 6: Moses Meets God Face to Face

As the deer pants for the stream of water, so my soul
pants for you, O God. My soul thirsts for God, for the
living God. When can I go and meet with God? (Ps.
42:1)

Chapter 7: Elijah Hears the Gentle Whisper

"Go lie down and say, 'Speak LORD, for
your servant is listening.'" (1 Sam. 3:9)

Chapter 8: Jesus Hears His Father's Voice

"Come with me by yourselves to a quiet place
and get some rest." (Mark 6:31)

Part IV—The Practical Process of Achieving Stillness with God

Chapter 9: How to Be Still Physically

1. David Lloyd and Ernest L. Rossi, eds., *Ultradian Rhythms in Life Processes: An Inquiry into Fundamental Principles of Chronobiology and Psychobiology* (London: Springer-Verlag, 1992). This book contains the many detailed, scientific studies pertaining to our ultradian rhythms.

2. Ernest Rossi, *The 20-minute Break: Reduce Stress, Maximize Performance, And Improve Health and Emotional Well-Being Using the New Science of Ultradian Rhythms* (Los Angeles: Jeremy P. Tarcher, Inc., 1991), ix.

3. Ibid., 98.

Chapter 10: How to Be Still Emotionally

"Sorrow may endure for a night, but
joy comes in the morning." (Ps. 30:5)

Chapter 11: How to Be Still Spiritually

1. St. John of the Cross was a sixteenth century Carmelite monk. He died in 1591 and was named a doctor of the Catholic Church by Pope Pius XI in 1921. Some of his major works on the spiritual life are *Ascent on Mount Carmel, Dark Night of the Soul, Spiritual Canticle,* and *Living Flame of Love.*

2. St. John of the Cross. 1964. *The Collected Works of St. John of the Cross*, trans. Kieran Kavanaugh and Otilio Rodriguez, Garden City, NY: Doubleday. p. 365.

Part V—From the Rooftop to the Mountaintop

Chapter 12: Transforming Results

Our hearts were made for Thee, oh Lord, and restless will they ever be until at last we rest in Thee. St. Augustine

Part VI—An Out of This World Experience

Chapter 13: Praying Intimately

1. Donald Bloesch, in *Men's Devotional Bible* (Grand Rapids: Zondervan, 1997), 153.
2. Leith Anderson, *Praying to the God You Can Trust* (Minneapolis: Bethany House Publishers, 1998), 63.
3. Richard Foster, *Prayer: Finding the Heart's True Home* (San Francisco: Harper, 1992), 3.
4. C. Welton Gaddy, *A Love Affair with God* (Nashville: Broadman & Holman Publishers, 1995), 60.
5. Donald Bloesch, in *Men's Devotional Bible* (Grand Rapids: Zondervan, 1997), 153.

Chapter 14: Fast and Focus

1. James F. Balch and Phyllis A. Balch, C.N.C., *Prescription for Nutritional Healing*, 2d ed. (Garden City, N.Y.: Avery Publishing Group, 1997), 548.
2. T. Lewis, *The International Standard Bible Encyclopedia* [Electronic Database, 1996], Available from Biblesoft.
3. J. Pedersen, *The New Unger's Bible Dictionary* (Chicago: Moody Press, 1988) [Electronic Database, 1996], Available from Biblesoft.

4. (Hippocrates, M.D., 460? -370? B.C., Father of Western Medicine)

5. Joel Fuhrman, *Fasting and Eating for Health: A Medical Doctor's Program for Conquering Disease* (from the Internet, 1995).

6. Joseph Pizzorno and Michael T. Murray, *Encyclopedia of Natural Medicine,* rev. 2d ed., (Rockland, Calif.: Prima Publishing, 1998), 124.

7. Elmer Towns, Fasting for Spiritual Breakthrough (Ventura, Calif.: Regal, 1996).

Chapter 15: The Penetrating Word

"Do not conform any longer to the pattern of the world, but be transformed by the renewing of your mind."
(Rom. 12:2)

Order Form for the Book and the Tape

1. **Book**: *TRANSFORMED: INTIMACY WITH GOD*

2. **Tape**: *Intimacy With God*—side one, *Resting With God*—side two. Audio Cassette Tape. Have a 20-minute, quiet time with Jesus. (See page 17 for a description of the tape.) Here is how one person described the material on the tape:

"The first class I attended that we focused on God, you spoke, taking us on a walk through fields, describing colors and items of colors. It was a beautiful walk and pretty clear for me. At the end of the path we walked into a forest and sat by a tree. This is where my emotions took over—that Jesus should come and sit with me—ME! —Humbled me beyond my dreams. I could see Him there; I could feel Him hold me, asking for my troubles and pains. It was beautiful. I try to remind myself since; that Jesus is walking with me—always! Thank you Anthony."

How did you hear about the book? _____

How has the book helped you? _____

_____

What is one main lesson you have learned from the book?

_____

_____

How can the book be improved? _____

_____

To Order, complete the form below and send it in with a check or money order.

----------------------(PRINT CLEARLY)----------------------

Name: _____

Telephone: _____

Address:_____

City: _____State:_____Zip: _____

Quantity of the Book: _____ X $15.99   = _____

Quantity of Audio Cassette Tape_____ X $7.00 = _____

Add 6% sales tax for orders shipped to PA: _____

Shipping Charges:
One book: $3.50, 2 to 5 books: $5.00,
6 to 10 books: $7.00   = _____

One tape: $1.00, 2 to 5 tapes: $2.50,
6 to 10 tapes: $4.00   = _____

Total Cost: _____

Further discounts for larger quantities.

E-mail: afische101@aol.com

Mail Check and Order Form to:

Alpha Omega Counseling Center, Inc.
475 Philadelphia Ave., PO Box 66
Reading, PA 19607

Personal Notes and Comments

Personal Notes and Comments